ANNUAL 1

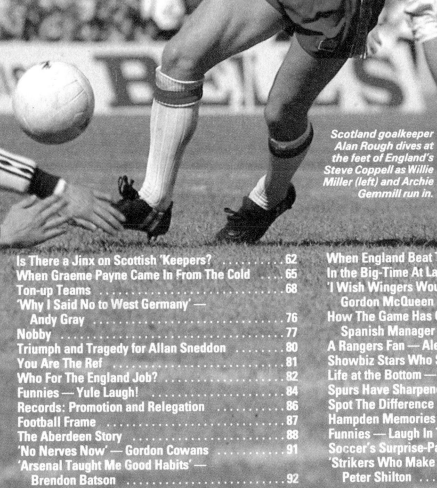

Scotland goalkeeper Alan Rough dives at the feet of England's Steve Coppell as Willie Miller (left) and Archie Gemmill run in.

Is There a Jinx on Scottish 'Keepers? 62
When Graeme Payne Came In From The Cold .. 65
Ton-up Teams 68
'Why I Said No to West Germany' —
    Andy Gray 76
Nobby 77
Triumph and Tragedy for Allan Sneddon 80
You Are The Ref 81
Who For The England Job? 82
Funnies — Yule Laugh! 84
Records: Promotion and Relegation 86
Football Frame 87
The Aberdeen Story 88
'No Nerves Now' — Gordon Cowans 91
'Arsenal Taught Me Good Habits' —
    Brendon Batson 92

When England Beat Two World Champions 93
In the Big-Time At Last — Paul McGhee 97
'I Wish Wingers Would Fly Again' —
    Gordon McQueen 98
How The Game Has Changed — by a Famous
    Spanish Manager 102
A Rangers Fan — Alex McDonald 105
Showbiz Stars Who Support Soccer 106
Life at the Bottom — Bryan Hamilton 110
Spurs Have Sharpened Steve Archibald 111
Spot The Difference 112
Hampden Memories — Derek Johnstone 113
Funnies — Laugh In The New Year 116
Soccer's Surprise-Packets 120
'Strikers Who Make My Job Extra-Difficult' —
    Peter Shilton 124

© IPC Magazines Ltd 1981 SBN 85037-671-8

£2·25

No pocket calculator, however sophisticated, could assess the full weight of Kevin Keegan's contribution to English football since he came into the big time as a wide-eyed, frail youth at Liverpool.

He blossomed rapidly, first under Bill Shankly's direction and then in Bob Paisley's Red coven to become a legend on Merseyside and go on to reach even wider frontiers with his dazzling exploits in Europe.

The greatest compliment Keegan could be given is to say that he burst on the scene like a comet to offer magic on a First Division stage shorne of much of its superstar material in the drab Seventies.

Keegan had been a Liverpool player only four months when he first played against Bobby Moore, captain of West Ham and the England team that won the World Cup.

Here was his first real opportunity to see whether he would ever attain the levels England's great captain had achieved.

Bill Shankly, Liverpool's manager and something of a Messiah himself, stood in the dressing-room passage to inspect the opposition. Nothing escaped him. He noted how they dressed, if they had shaved, whether they were trying to hide an injury, how their hair was groomed, if they looked tired.

He studied West Ham and beckoned young Keegan to the corner of the dressing-room. "I've seen that Bobby Moore," he rasped. "Big bags under his eyes. Limping. He's been out in a night-club last night again, son.

KEVIN KEEGAN The 'Mighty Mouse' with a lion's roar

Kevin shows he not only possesses ball skill, but the strength to deal with a determined challenge.

"He's scared stiff of playing against you. You'll run him silly."

It was the same year that Moore and three other West Ham players had been carpeted for visiting a Blackpool night-club on the eve of an F.A. Cup-tie.

Shankly had not wasted the opportunity to lift the morale of the Liverpool team.

That moment when their lives crossed was a significant milestone in the Seventies — the flower of English football in the twilight of his career, the new superstar bursting on the scene.

After Kevin had run himself ragged helping Liverpool beat West Ham, he realised he'd been a victim of Shanks' "kidology".

"Bobby's still a great player," the manager said. "He didn't put a foot wrong, Kevin. You helped us show we are the better team."

Keegan maintains that England spent too long replacing the superstars who had won the World Cup, especially the little toothless hero of the hour, Nobby Stiles.

"Nobby is a wonderful wee man,

rightly one of football's most popular characters, but no one seemed to notice that his type of ferocious ball-winning was undergoing some sophisticated development on the Continent, particularly in Germany and Italy.

"They saw the need for a ball-winning marker as used by England, but decided that the job should be done by a dual-purpose player with the skill to move up as an inside-forward as well as the concentration of power to shadow and tackle.

"Bonhof of Germany and Tardelli of Italy immediately spring to mind as fulfilling that role, while the outstanding example of Benetti of Italy, who can be as delicate in placing a pass as he is mighty in winning the ball. With that kind of all-rounder in midfield, the Continentals had 12 men to our 11."

It remains one of Kevin Keegan's

During his spell in West Germany, scoring goals for Hamburger SV, Kevin captained England regularly.

favourite tales to record that the eventual replacement for Stiles was Peter Storey, the destructive Arsenal midfield player, who once revealed his attitude and limitations by saying: "If it wasn't for people like me, the Sugar Plum Fairy could play centre-forward."

Storey, bereft of most of the skills of that glittering array of European talent aforementioned, won no fewer than 18 England caps.

"I look on that era as a turn down the wrong road," Keegan maintains.

But that was the atmosphere he had to conquer in a decade when fear amongst managers was commonplace and many finished on the scrapheap. Much of the fun went out of the game and it reached an all-time low, according to Keegan, when Brian Clough made a speech at a dinner in honour of Peter Lorimer of Leeds United.

"It was meant to be a nice evening," Keegan recalls. "Then Clough stood up. Instead of proposing the toast, he announced 'I'm off to the lavatory' — and he didn't return for nearly a quarter of an hour.

"It still amazes me how patiently everyone waited. The toast was 'Peter Lorimer, Yorkshire sports personality of the Year' and, regardless of whether he thought Lorimer deserved the award or not, Clough had agreed to propose it. But his speech criticised Lorimer, the Leeds United Club and the Leeds players."

It is a measure of Kevin Keegan's immense talent that he managed to escape from the quagmire of mediocrity holding English football in a stranglehold in the Seventies to win his first England cap against Wales, at Cardiff in 1972, and countless honours

with Liverpool, including the European Cup in 1977.

When soccer historians assess Keegan's contribution, they might well judge him as the saviour of English football from the playing point of view, with Ron Greenwood, England's manager, the man who steered a troubled football land back on to the right rails.

If Greenwood's appointment as England manager swept away years of negative thinking, Keegan has done his bit for the cause too.

"His (Greenwood's) theme is 'We tried defence for four years and it didn't work. So let's attack'."

Keegan warms to the former West Ham manager's refreshing lead. He never truly believed in Don Revie's "dossier" inspired regime though he admits that he grew closer to Revie towards the end of the former Leeds United's boss's reign.

His respect for Greenwood can be measured by the way "Mighty Mouse" has flung himself into the cause of rescuing England. While many players were shrugging off a long season of physical exertion in the summer of 1979, Kevin flew in from his home in Hamburg, West Germany, to help make a coaching film at Bisham Abbey for the Football Association.

He rightly believed the England captain should be seen to play a major part in the production of a film that would influence thousands of youngsters.

Nothing appears to be too much trouble for Kevin. He once played for Hamburg at Frankfurt in the afternoon, then drove 115 miles to Cologne and played again that evening in a five-a-side tournament with Allan Simonsen, European Footballer of the Year. Later that night he flew by private jet to Gatwick, England. The following day he kept nine appointments, weary but smiling.

It was typical of him to shock the football world by signing for Southampton in a secret deal struck in 1980 with Lawrie McMenemy that would have won the approval of Eamonn Andrews' "This Is Your Life" team.

He had played superbly for great clubs in England's First Division and with Hamburg in the highly competitive German Bundesliga. Now, he was coming down market to join Southampton, a club with brave ambitions but short on tradition.

"It's the end of Keegan. A mistake," muttered some critics disapprovingly.

What happened? Keegan shrugged off a prolonged injury which handicapped him severely in his first season at The Dell to lead the Saints to the threshold of an exciting new era.

"You've climbed Everest," commented Bill Shankly when Keegan first won Europe's top honour. Some believe Kevin Keegan will scale other summits before he is finished.

England manager 1990? Anything is possible for the maestro.

5

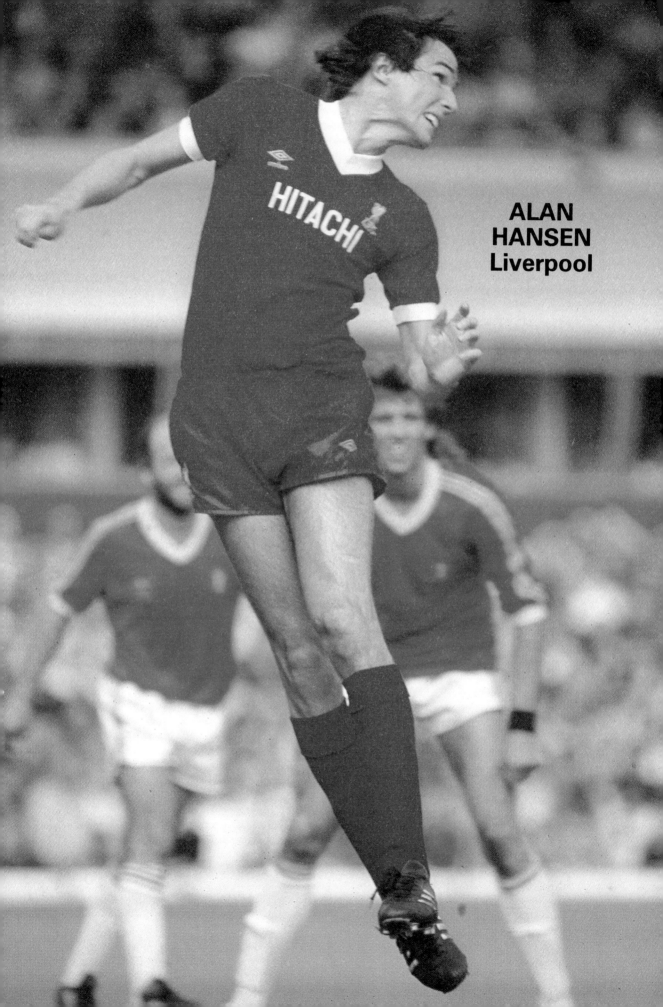

ALAN HANSEN
Liverpool

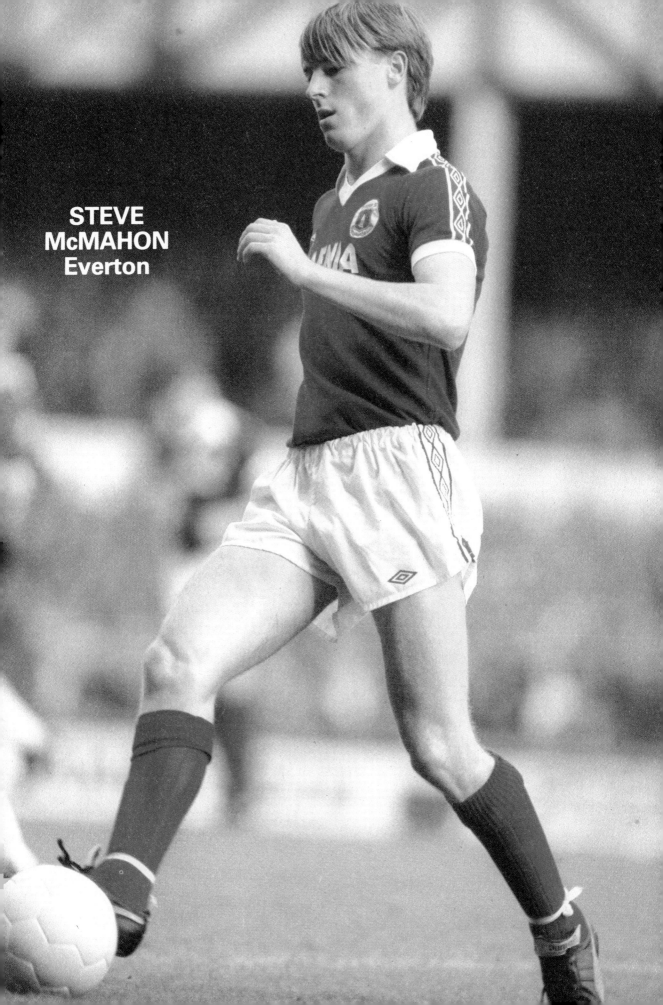

STEVE
McMAHON
Everton

'Misfits' who

Sir Stanley Matthews can't have a more embarrassing memory than the day he called a young factory worker into the manager's office at Port Vale and told him: "You'll never make a professional footballer, son."

The player, of course, was Ray Kennedy. He took Sir Stan's words so seriously that he went on to win the Double with Arsenal and now has more medals than the average Chelsea pensioner.

It's easy to laugh at Matthews' mistake today. But football is littered with players who have failed to make an impression at one club and gone on to stardom at another. In football, one manager's misfit can be another manager's maestro.

Sir Stanley wasn't to know how rapidly Kennedy was going to progress, nor how determinedly he was going to react to those stinging remarks.

Says Kennedy: "I wanted to prove him wrong, just as I was anxious to prove people wrong when they said that my move from Arsenal to Liverpool was the end for me. I took a long time to establish myself in the Anfield team but I knew I had the ability.

"When I was dropped by England at one time it had the same effect on me. It motivated me to get back in the team and prove myself."

Worth a Place

Kennedy's team-mate Graeme Souness is equally determined when his ability as a player is questioned. He kept insisting at Spurs as a youngster that he was worth a place in the first team.

But the chance was so long coming that he eventually moved on to Middlesbrough, where it was assumed he'd disappear from the public eye forever.

Instead, he helped a resurgent Middlesbrough back to the top — and ended up a star at Anfield and for Scotland.

Clubs like Spurs, who are always likely to splash out big sums on star players, know that they run the risk of disenchanted youngsters by doing so.

Noel Brotherston left them after just one first team game and is now one of the leading players at Blackburn.

He says: "I've no regrets, but at Spurs it seemed that the young players didn't get a fair crack of the whip. The big money signings went straight into the team but youngsters got so far and no further.

"When you realise that you are not going to make progress, you have to decide whether it wouldn't be better to move on to somewhere you're wanted. It took me a while to adjust, though, and it's only now that I'm really starting to enjoy my football."

There are plenty of youngsters who move on without making one first team appearance for their club — and go on to be a huge success elsewhere.

George Berry served his apprenticeship at Ipswich but with the likes of Kevin Beattie and Allan Hunter around, he never looked like making it to senior level.

The big central defender decided to take his chances elsewhere. He moved on to Wolves and made such an impact that he was picked for Wales. "It was unbelievable. I never dreamed that I would play international football."

Similarly, Phil Boyer didn't dream that he'd play for England one day when Derby, for whom he'd never played a League match, dispatched him to York.

But his success in a town better known for its racecourse than its football ground led to further, successful transfers to Bournemouth, Norwich and Southampton. And that one cap for England in 1976.

Brendon Batson never made much of an impression at Arsenal, even though he won half a dozen League appearances.

He seemed to be on a one-way road out of the big time when he agreed to join Cambridge. But his performances in the Fourth Division inspired Ron

Ray Kennedy (left) disproved a manager's prediction that he'd never make a professional footballer by winning honours with Arsenal and Liverpool. Brendon Batson (right) returned to the First Division to star for West Brom. Neil Brotherston (duelling below right with West Ham's Frank Lampard) only had one game for Spurs, yet has shone with Blackburn Rovers.

made good

Atkinson to sign him for First Division West Brom.

Some players just seem to need a familiar environment in order to produce their best form. Derek Hales, for instance, who has had two incredibly successful spells with Charlton interspersed with lack-lustre spells at Derby and West Ham.

Loyal Servant

Other players seem to need managerial inspiration. There can't be a better example than John McGovern, who has served under Brian Clough at Hartlepool, Derby, Leeds and Nottingham Forest. The one awful period during all that was between Clough leaving Leeds and his return to sign his loyal servant.

Says McGovern: "People think I must know Brian Clough better than anyone else but it's not true. Our relationship is purely a professional one.

"He does bring the best out of me but we don't mix off the field and I don't think we would be able to. Partly because I don't think we'd get on too well and partly because I feel there has to be some sort of distance between a manager and his players."

Leighton James is another player who seems to need a certain kind of environment to produce the form that is capable of destroying any defence. His brilliant performances at Burnley inspired Derby and then Q.P.R. to buy him.

But he wasn't really happy at either club, scoring just four goals in 27 games at Rangers and 15 in 67 at Derby. Now, back in familiar surroundings at Burnley, he is again turning in sparkling performances.

The success of all these so-called misfits goes to prove that atmosphere and conditions have much more effect on a footballer's performance than most managers probably realise.

It's something they might consider the next time they sit down to write a million pound cheque.

PETER WARD
Nottingham
Forest

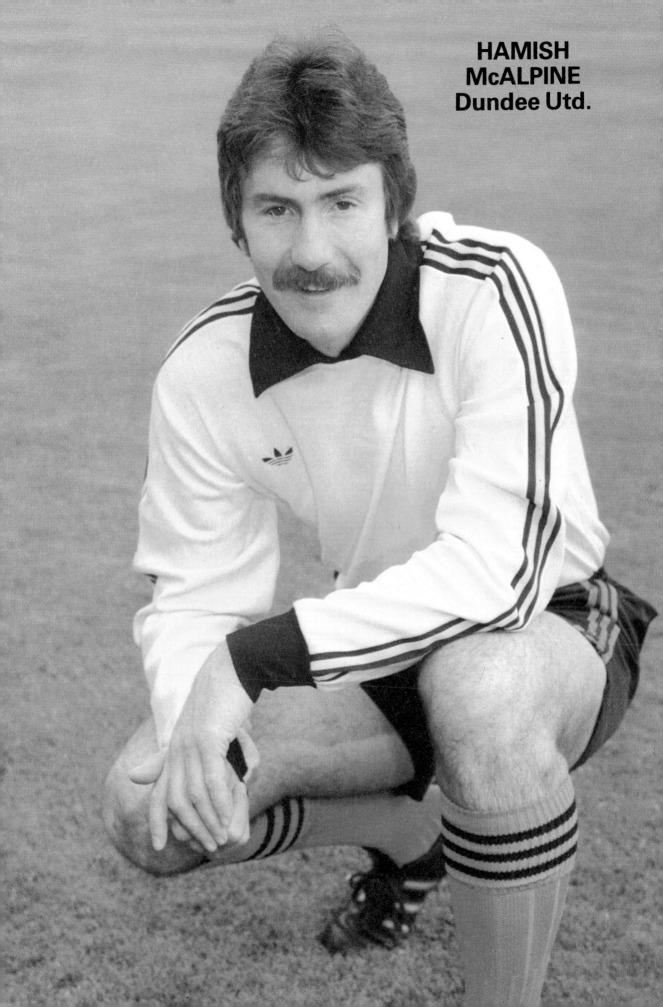

HAMISH McALPINE
Dundee Utd.

star-finding academy

Southampton boss Lawrie McMenemy is excited about the potential of Danny Wallace, another product of the Saints London-based star-finding academy.

They call it their London selection centre and already a talented group of youngsters have graduated from it through Southampton's junior and reserve team to the first team.

Danny Wallace has taken the same path trodden previously by Steve Williams, Austin Hayes and many others.

So McMenemy felt he was taking no risk when he decided to give Wallace his debut at the age of 16 ... against Manchester United at Old Trafford.

Reflecting on that exciting moment in November 1980, McMenemy recalls: "The lad had excited me in training. He lacks nothing in confidence and I wanted to have another look at him in a game."

Overall, the Saints manager can feel justifiably proud of a youth system which produces exciting young talent.

NEWS DESK

Compiled by BILL DAY

The youngest player to appear in the Scottish League was Ronnie Simpson who was 15 years 310 days old when he kept goal for Queen's Park v Hibernian on 17th August, 1946.

Simpson, in fact, made his first team debut againt Kilmarnock in the wartime Southern League on 11th August 1945 aged 14 years 304 days.

SWEEPERS CAN CLEAN UP

League clubs will be making greater use of sweepers at the heart of their defences in the next few years.

England manager Ron Greenwood (above) forecasts that the sweeper, or "libero", could become as commonplace as the striker or midfield man.

And he believes that if clubs will adopt this form of defence, which is used widely by European clubs, then England will benefit from the change in policy when they play matches.

"It seems to me that the most important single difference between our domestic football and that of say Italy or Germany is the comparative flatness of our defences," says Mr. Greenwood.

"Continental teams invariably use a sweeper, whereas our sides very rarely do. This has two main effects when our players step up to international football. The defenders have to cope with forwards whose skills have been sharpened by man-to-man marking, while the front men find it difficult to run at defences which have a great deal more depth than they are used to.

"I have no doubt we must adapt to be truly at home in the top levels of world football and learn what this style of play is all about."

Mr. Greenwood points out that Phil Thompson has already been employed in a "modified" sweeper role for the England team, a tribute to the Liverpool player's outstanding all-round abilities.

To those who suggest that a sweeper makes the game even more defensive, Greenwood argues: "You only have to look at Franz Beckenbauer to understand the attacking contribution a sweeper can make to his side.

"A little change from our clubs will do the international team a great deal of good," says Mr. Greenwood.

Will they take his advice?

Best finisher

Phil Boyer (centre right), Manchester City's striker, is the best finisher in the country.

That is the firm opinion held by Ivan Golac, Boyer's former team-mate in his Southampton days.

"It's not because we were friends, but Phil is so dangerous when he gets a chance," says Golac.

He was no doubt influenced by Boyer's record breaking goal-scoring feats at The Dell. He set a club record when scoring in 11 successive home games and was the Saints' top scorer for three seasons as he accumulated 62 League and Cup goals.

Southampton's loss is Manchester City's gain.

In the Russian Football League, clubs are allowed only eight drawn games a season. Any draw after that is still recorded but the point is not credited to that clubs' playing record.

Fans come first with Kev

Kevin Keegan's smiling face has been known to grace the odd advertisement or two, but one publicity session filmed at Wembley remains in the memory of those in the stadium.

Kevin was being photographed for Mitre Footballs, in front of the goal at the opposite end to the electronic scoreboard. At that moment a large party of schoolboys appeared in front of the Royal Box on a conducted tour of the stadium.

"Excuse me," whispered Kevin, and sprinted off to sign autographs for the youngsters.

That says a lot and helps to explain Kevin's deserved popularity.

One man with more than a casual interest in the forthcoming World Cup Finals in Spain is the Archbishop of Canterbury, Dr Robert Runcie.

The Archbishop revealed a passionate interest in football when he was the chief guest of the Football Association at the England-Switzerland World Cup qualifying game at Wembley in November 1980.

His enthusiasm for the game derives from schooldays in Liverpool, the city in which he was born in 1921.

Shock for Pele

Heard about the English woman who upset the great Brazilian superstar Pele (above) by switching on a two-bar electric fire at Aston Villa's ground?

It happened when Santos were invited to play a friendly at Villa Park in 1972.

The problem was that Santos, Pele's Brazilian League team, were scheduled to play the game at a time when the Midland area was threatened by a power strike.

Villa, one of England's more progressive clubs, bought a generator from Holland. They tested it to see if it would drive their floodlights on the Sunday before the game and it became clear that any overloading could cause a black-out.

Consequently, Villa cut down power to a minimum — no heating in the dressing-rooms, offices, or anywhere, not even hot water in the dressing-rooms.

The game attracted 54,000 fans but suddenly one of the floodlight towers went out during the game.

Pele threatened to walk off the pitch, accusing the club of deliberately dimming the lights behind the goal he was attacking in the second half.

Aston Villa carried out a post-mortem on the incident and it transpired that a lady, with no knowledge of the problem, had switched on a two-bar electric fire to keep warm. That simple incident took the loading over the critical point and put out the lights.

Pele apologised and all was forgiven.

The first time closed-circuit television was used to relay a soccer match in this country was in 1965 when some 10,000 fans packed into the Coventry City ground at Highfield to watch their team win at Cardiff, 120 miles away.

He went to school in Liverpool before gaining a scholarship to Oxford University.

During the War, he served with the Scots Guards Tank Regiment and took part in the Normandy landings.

He has always been a keen sportsman. He was captain of cricket at school, still plays tennis and retains a great love for football.

He is a regular after dinner speaker at sports functions.

The referee's whistle was first used on Nottingham Forest's ground in 1878.

STOKOE SAD

No one was sadder than Bob Stokoe when he read how one-time Sunderland star Billy Hughes was living on the dole and struggling to find a League club.

"It's a great pity because I liked Billy during our days at Roker together, but I tried to warn him about his lifestyle," recalls the former Sunderland manager.

"The way footballers live is very important because their stay at the top is so short. I told Billy to be careful about his friends and other personal matters or he would regret it in the future.

"Perhaps Billy couldn't cope with his success after the Cup win," says Stokoe, reflecting on the high-spot of his career when he managed Sunderland and led them to victory in the 1973 F.A. Cup Final.

Larry May, Leicester City's giant centre half, always celebrates Boxing Day by toasting himself with a glass of lemonade.

None of the hard liquor for Larry. Being a disciplined professional he sticks solely to soft drinks.

But why Boxing Day? Christmas Day is surely the time for a toast.

December 26th just happens to be Larry's birthday — and lemonade is his favourite soft drink.

Top twelve of managers

"Pop" Robson, whose career has taken him to Newcastle, West Ham twice, Sunderland (right) twice, and Carlisle, has rubbed shoulders with some great managers. It inspires him to produce a "Top Twelve", excluding those he has worked under.

Champion amongst an elite squad is Bob Paisley, Manager of Liverpool, who "makes one brilliant buy a year without ruffling the smooth Liverpool system. Quiet man, tough and very knowledgeable."

Bill Shankly, Paisley's predecessor, is second, the "best at firing up players before a match."

Brian Clough, Forest's outspoken boss, is given third place. Says Robson: "If you want success, you put up with the criticism and harsh words he doles out. Outspoken, intelligent, a great success in a short time."

Of Sir Alf Ramsey, the manager rated fourth in Robson's chart, he says: "Because of his fantastic success at Ipswich and the World Cup win of which I'm proud."

Others are:- 5 Bill Nicholson, 6 Sir Matt Busby, 7 Jock Stein, 8 Don Revie, 9 Bobby Robson, 10 Bertie Mee, 11 Harry Catterick, 12 Ron Saunders.

Quote of the year from Ted Croker (above) the Football Association secretary: "I have the greatest respect for Mrs Thatcher, but whether she likes it or not, in most countries of the world the taxi drivers won't know her — but they will know Bobby Charlton!"

Emlyn Hughes admits the appointment of Ron Greenwood as England manager had him worried.

"We thought he was a textbook man," says Hughes, who won 62 caps.

"But nothing could be further from the truth," Hughes observes. "He is intelligent, certainly, but he talks players' language.

"He has brought some pride back into English football, and he concerns himself about the game at every level."

Hughes also offers some interesting opinions on the other England managers he served in a distinguished international career.

Alf Ramsey? "He was a players' manager, he spoke our language, he was one of us, and we respected him a great deal."

Don Revie? "Whatever you may say about him, and I have said a lot like everyone else, he was a dedicated professional who always wanted to win. And he was a good organiser."

Joe Mercer? "Joe was the funniest man I ever met. He made the players feel relaxed, and made playing for England a pleasure again."

Terry Venables, manager at Queens Park Rangers, became the first player to hold England caps at five levels — school, youth, amateur, Under-23 and full international.

He achieved the honour at the age of 21 when he played for Chelsea.

RESPECT FOR COVENTRY

Ron Atkinson, manager of West Bromwich Albion, has always been generous in his praise of players and other clubs.

His attitude illustrates the new-found spirit in football, which should see the sport rise above the problems which beset it in the 1970s.

Here is Ron talking about Midland rivals Coventry City: "Many aspects of Coventry and the way they try to do things on and off the field, impresses me greatly.

"Their organisation epitomises how a football club should be run with facilities always to the fore — and their football has kept pace with it.

"In my opinion the progress they have made as a club, through the eras of Jimmy Hill, Noel Cantwell and Gordon Milne, has made them a very respected First Division club."

TONY GODDEN
W.B.A.

The old and the new . . .Wolves'
Emlyn Hughes and Mark
Hateley of Coventry City.

CLUB RECORDS

Quick entry for Chelsea

If Fulham had accepted an offer from the owner of Stamford Bridge to rent the ground for their home matches there might never have been a Chelsea club. Fulham rejected the offer and so it was decided to form a football club to play on the new ground. Chelsea came into being and, unlike every other Football League club, did not kick a ball in any competition before being admitted into the Second Division of the League. Indeed, they became League members only a little over two months after coming into existence in 1905.

"Lancashire ring"

Towards the end of 1902-03, when Blackburn Rovers were struggling to avoid relegation from the First Division, their 3—0 win against Everton at Goodison Park caused quite a furore. The "Athletic News" suggested that "It is evident the football public entertain a profound impression that Everton were generous to their Lancashire neighbours." There was talk about a "Lancashire Ring" in which the clubs from that county helped each other when circumstances so demanded. Grimsby Town, who were relegated that season, complained so bitterly that a Commission of the F.A. and the Football League held an investigation at which all members of the Everton team were in attendance. They were, however, given the benefit of the doubt and the sole responsibility for any irregularity that may have occurred was heaped upon the Blackburn Rovers secretary who was suspended for life. A record Rovers hardly relish holding.

Comebacks

Among all present members of the Football League only two have previously resigned from the competition and both are from the Potteries — Port Vale and Stoke City.

Port Vale (or Burlem Port Vale as they were then known) finished in 16th place (out of 20) in the Second Division in 1906-07, but they were in difficult financial straits and tendered their resignation during the summer. They were replaced by Oldham Athletic who had only a couple of weeks earlier failed to gain election to both the Football League and the Southern League.

It was only 12 months later that Stoke resigned their membership of the League after finishing 10th in the Second Division. The club declared that

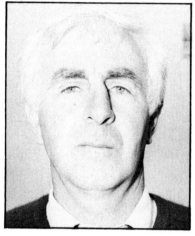

public apathy had forced their resignation; only three shareholders having turned up for their Annual Meeting. Tottenham Hotspur were elected in their place.

Both Stoke and Port Vale returned to the Second Division in 1919, Stoke coming in at the start of 1919-20, while Port Vale took over the fixtures of the Leeds City club which had been wound up in October.

Tea total

In their earliest days Birmingham City (then known as Small Heath Alliance) entertained their players to tea after every match. It was a club rule that the cost of the tea should not exceed 6d (2½p) per man.

Hit for ten — twice

Rotherham United is the only club among present members of the Football League to have had 10 or more goals scored against them twice in a single season. In 1928-29 they were beaten 11—1 by Bradford City (away) and 10—1 by South Shields (away). Both games were in Division Three (N).

Keeping it in the family

Not many clubs in the British Isles have been managed by both father and son of the same family, but this has happened twice at Fulham.

Harry Bradshaw was their manager from 1904 to 1924 and really helped put them on the football map. His son, Joe, took over in 1926 and remained until 1931.

In April 1949 they appointed Bill Dodgin team-manager and he held the post until September 1953. A little over 15 years later, in December 1968, Fulham appointed his son, Bill junior, (left) as team-manager and he occupied the position until June 1972.

Continued after K.O.

Reading survived a 7—0 defeat in the F.A. Cup to pass into the next round! This was in 1891-92 when, following their heavy defeat by Southampton St. Mary's (the present Southampton club), they entered an appeal on the grounds that the winners had included two ineligible players. The appeal was upheld but in the next Round Reading were heavily defeated again, this time 8—2 by Clifton (Bristol).

On the move

Few clubs have played on as many different home grounds as Queens Park Rangers who have had at least a dozen. In addition to which they moved from Loftus Road to the White City in 1931; back to Loftus Road in 1933, and had another spell at the White City (1962-63) before returning to Loftus Road. (Below: match action between Q.P.R. and Shrewsbury Town at Loftus Road).

ARMSTRONG'S LONG-PLAYING RECORD

David Armstrong made history during the 1980/81 season. During the autumn he was injured and missed a game...breaking a sequence of almost 400 games that dated back to March 24th, 1973.

In these days of competitive soccer, with a minimum of about 50 games a season even for unsuccessful clubs, to avoid injury for over seven years is truly remarkable.

Armstrong is still only in his mid-twenties. He's one of those players who you think must be approaching the twilight of his career because he's been around so long. It's simply that he fought his way into the Boro team as a teenager — and stayed there.

The likeable Armstrong, who had a testimonial last year, can't put his finger on the reason for his long playing record.

"I love football," he says, "which must help. I'd play twice a week throughout the season if I could. I was, naturally, sorry to break my unbeaten run, but I can't complain.

"I don't really think about records... how many games I've played. I just get on with the game. I realise I'm lucky to have avoided injury. Most of all I realise I'm lucky to be paid to do something I would be doing for nothing were I not a professional.

"I tend not to look forward or backward. I take each match as it comes — each day as it comes, really.

Quick Healer

"I've had knocks, although they haven't been serious. Maybe I'm a quick healer. Perhaps I've played when I haven't been totally 100 per cent fit. I've never let the team down, though. In a game of such physical contact it's possibly true to say that every footballer is always carrying some sort of strain or bruise.

"What I've *never* done is to play just to keep my record. When it came to the crunch last season and I was injured badly enough to keep me sidelined I accepted it.

"I've also been fortunate that both Jack Charlton and John Neal have kept me in the team even when I wasn't playing well. Some players have been dropped under similar circumstances. I seemed to play my way through a bad patch.

"I was a little worried when Jack arrived. A big name player with Leeds...we didn't know what to expect."

Under Charlton, Boro won the Second Division Championship by a distance. Since then they've become brighter under John Neal, while Charlton, who thought he'd gone as far as he could at Ayresome Park, has found success with Sheffield Wednesday.

Armstrong used to be a winger. These days he's found more in midfield, although always looking to go wide and break down the left wing.

Armstrong has deservedly won England B honours. During the summer of 1980 he even won a full England cap, although to many people it was a 'B' game.

"We played in Australia and it was made a full international by the Football Association.

"Whatever others may say, I have an England cap and no one can take that honour away from me."

The Boro star has been a model professional and deserved his recognition.

Perhaps he didn't play for England at Wembley or in the World Cup. But surely no one will begrudge him the solitary cap he had to go Down Under to win.

David Armstrong (Left) duels with Osvaldo Ardiles of Spurs.

'Keepers are a special breed'

Goalkeepers are born and not made. It took an ultimatum from my youth club leader, school sportsmaster Frank Mott, to force me to realise the truth of that old football saying.

I'd always fancied myself as a striker, scoring goals not saving them, until Frank — with whom I still keep in touch — pointed out that I possessed all the natural abilities of a goalkeeper, and that unless I agreed to play between the sticks for our Skegness youth club side in a Cup Final, then he intended to drop me!

At first I was bitterly disappointed. My dream of becoming a second Bobby Charlton had been shattered by Frank's statement.

But after our 4—3 win — Frank said we'd have lost 12—4 without my services — I realised how right he'd been in his assessment, and was soon relishing playing in the "number one" position so much I could hardly credit I'd seen myself in an entirely different role.

Mind you, I never imagined I'd go on to become a regular with a record Championship-winning club like Liverpool and also with England.

From the self-knowledge sparked off by Frank, and from observation, I'm convinced 'keepers are a very special breed with built-in talent which no coach in the world can reproduce. All he can do is bring it out, develop it to the full.

So many young, aspiring 'keepers write to me for help I've decided to devote this article to passing on advice in the hope I can help at least one reader to significantly improve his game and perhaps make it his profession.

One requirement is a good, strong physique to withstand the battering you have to take from physical challenges, dealing with shots that often come at you with the power of a steam hammer, and from hurling yourself around on surfaces which vary from concrete-hard in summer and mid-winter to marsh-like in rain or during a thaw.

It's also regarded as beneficial to be tall, around six-foot, but there are many exceptions who have made the grade, such as Laurie Sivell of Ipswich Town.

The first three letters of the alphabet — ABC — stand for three important qualities: agility, anticipation, bravery and confidence in your own ability.

Probably the most vital talent of all is a good pair of hands, the main difference between a 'keeper and an outfield player.

Because a 'keeper isn't called upon to do much running, many people are under the impression he doesn't have to be as fit as his team-mates. This is a fallacy. In fact, I believe he should be fitter to fulfill a role that in many ways is more demanding.

At Liverpool, we 'keepers train as hard — perhaps harder — than the rest, and I'll briefly outline a typical schedule which you might care to follow.

We start with a warm-up, which involves lapping our Melwood training ground at a comfortable pace, sometimes dribbling with the ball.

Then we 'keepers separate from the others for specialised exercises aimed at strengthening the stomach muscles. Sitting on the ground we catch balls thrown above, and to either side, of our heads, for around three minutes.

' The Assassin'

Next, there's a test of agility. We stand facing a wall with a trainer behind us. He hurls the ball at the wall and we have to catch it as it rebounds at different angles.

The following exercise is one we dread if we're feeling a bit below par, perhaps because of a late night or a hard match.

Standing in the centre of a triangle of posts, we have to defend the "goals" between two sticks as players stationed at each stick take it in turns to shoot.

We round off the session with conventional shooting practice and a five-a-side game in which I'm allowed to play as a forward. I charge about so much, tackling like mad, I'm nicknamed "The Assassin".

I assure you, a morning at Melwood takes more out of me physically than a 90-minute League game. It's the mental pressure, imposed by intense concentration, that can leave me drained after a hard-fought match. Playing behind such a superb, well-

Laurie Sivell — small but top class.

drilled team as Liverpool means I'm out of action for long periods and it requires a great effort to prevent my attention from straying.

Now for some tips on the fundamentals of keeping goal. My first is — keep your body behind the ball and your legs closed, particularly when dealing with low shots. I paid a dear price for forgetting this golden rule at Hampden Park, against Scotland in 1976.

Kenny Dalglish, then a Celtic player, came racing through with the ball. I went to cover the near post. But Kenny mis-kicked, the ball bobbled over the turf — and clean through my legs to give the Scots victory over England!

It was my greatest mistake — a night-mare which thankfully stopped haunting me shortly afterwards when I helped Liverpool beat Bruges on aggregate to win the U.E.F.A. Cup for the second time.

What do I consider to be the most diffi-cult part of a 'keeper's job? Dealing with crosses, a task which if you can master it will give your defenders great confidence in you.

You need to become expert at judging the speed and trajectory of a cross so as to decide exactly when to move to make an interception. It's also important never to take your eyes off the ball or to change your mind.

And avoid finding yourself flat-footed, needing to make a standing jump. Chances are then a leaping forward will get his head

A nightmare for Ray — when he allowed Scotland's Kenny Dalglish to slot the ball between his legs and into the Hampden Park net. (Left): A few days later he wiped out that memory by helping his Liverpool team-mates to beat Bruges on aggregate to win the U.E.F.A. Cup.

higher than your hands.

I'll now pass on a piece of advice I received from Ted Sagar, a legendary Everton 'keeper, who coined the expression: "Be the boss"!

You must command the six-yard box, and preferably the entire penalty area as well, positioning your defenders so they can mark the opposition without impeding your interception of the ball.

This is especially important at corners, a set-piece move which favours attackers. I prefer to station a player at each post to deal with a header or shot into either corner, another in the centre of the six-yard box, and a fourth two or three yards in front of the near post to cope with a ball driven into that position.

The low cross or corner is difficult, and I've spent many hours perfecting my technique of diving for the ball and ensuring it stays glued to my hands. Drop it and there'll be a hungry opponent ready and waiting to chip into goal.

If I find I can't reach a high cross or corner, because I've either misjudged it or am "crowded out" by players, I'll risk punching the ball clear. If possible, I'll punch high to prevent it dropping in or around the box for someone to try a first-time shot.

Punching is very common on the Continent. Spain's 'keeper, Arconada, did a great deal of it during our friendly against his country in Barcelona in 1980, when we won 2—0, but in my view he would have been more effective if he'd caught the ball and started moves with well-placed kicks or throws.

At Liverpool I am expected to initiate attacks in this way.

When I first arrived at Anfield I spent a great deal of time perfecting my kicking and throwing, and I like to think I've played a vital part in many of the goals we've scored in all sorts of competitions.

At first I had trouble with dead-ball kicks, until Gordon Banks, England's great 'keeper in the 1966 World Cup winning team, advised me that instead of directly running at the ball I should run in a curve. Since then I have achieved greater distance and accuracy.

Dealing with dead-ball kicks needs a good understanding between you and your defenders. When the ball is at a narrow angle to the goal, the general practice is to place two players in your "wall", but if the kick is to be taken square-on you could need five for the proper cover.

Saving a penalty is a bonus. The odds are all on the side of the kicker. Here, I usually gamble on going to the side the kicker prefers, noted from watching TV or from advice from my coaches.

As a rough guide, the kicker will usually follow his natural kicking action: a right-footed player will tend to hit the ball to your right, and vice versa.

Finally, being quick off your line can add an extra dimension to your team, as I do with Liverpool. It enables you to act as a second "sweeper", to rush out and thwart an attacker who has broken through the defence and is chasing the ball towards your goal.

My most memorable save of this kind was against Borussia Moenchengladbach in the 1977 European Cup Final in Rome when I rocketted out of my area to dispossess danger man Steilike, to prevent the Germans from taking the lead.

History shows we went on to win the Cup for the first time in Liverpool's history, by 3—1.

You probably won't find this type of "save" mentioned in the text books. But then neither will you find other unconventional ones, such as Arsenal's Pat Jennings' unique method of saving with his feet!

Allowance must always be made for individuality. Many of the world's most famous players break the rules, yet achieve remarkable results.

The game must never be taken over by players who all think and play alike.

So whatever your position, try to do things the right way for you!

21

IT'S AGONY

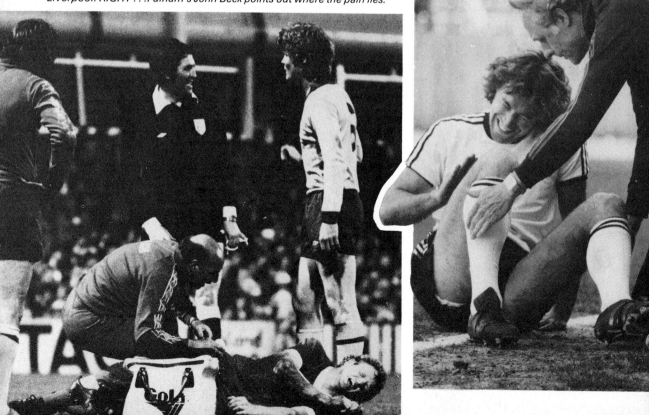

TOP OF PAGE . . . Arsenal's £1 million full-back, Kenny Sansom, writhes in agony after a fierce tackle. ABOVE . . . England skipper Kevin Keegan receives treatment from Southampton trainer Lew Chatterley. BELOW . . . Willie Young (right) has a word with referee Keith Hackett while Arsenal team-mate Pat Jennings looks over the injured David Fairclough of Liverpool. RIGHT . . . Fulham's John Beck points out where the pain lies.

'I don't rule by fear'
BRIAN CLOUGH

Brian Clough. Controversial. Likeable. Despicable. Successful. The adjectives could go on forever about the man who is arguably England's most successful manager at League level in the history of our game. Like him or hate him, you can't ignore Cloughie.

Brian Clough, the man who has won the Championship with two different clubs: Derby County and Nottingham Forest. He's also won the League Cup and European Cup twice with Forest.

He can be charming or rude, depending on how the mood takes him. Usually, though, he is polite to those who deserve politeness and rude to those who deserve abuse.

He'll think nothing of keeping someone waiting for half an hour; but if you're late expect to be torn off a strip.

Cloughie is a complex character and perhaps the reasons behind his success are that no one really knows the man.

There is another, less publicised side to Brian Clough. Last season he was commended by the Nottingham police after saving a man's life. Clough was driving along in his car over a bridge and noticed a man about to commit suicide. He stood there and talked to the man for an hour before someone called the police. Clough won't tell what he said to the man — but it worked.

Again he was in his car when he saw two 14-year-old boys hitch-hiking. He stopped, asked them where they were going and was told by the teenagers that they were running away from home. Clough bundled them in his car and took them back to their parents.

He seriously thought about standing as Labour candidate for Stretford (Manchester) against the Conservative Winston Churchill, son of the late Sir Winston Churchill.

'Too late'

"I would have loved to have beaten him," says Clough. "In the end I turned down the offer. When I was 35 I was a real fanatic and wanted to change the world. Now, it's too late.

"It's the same with football. Forest is my last job. When you're in your mid-40's it's harder to start all over again somewhere else. I have 2½ years of my contract left.

"My big regret is that Peter Taylor and I have never managed a big club. We've won the title with two small clubs. Can you imagine what we would have done at Liverpool or Manchester United?

"I can't honestly say what the future holds for me. The England job is out of the question. My wife, Barbara, often asks me what I'd do without football and I can't answer her. Perhaps something will come along that I fancy doing, even if it's working in a park."

Those who have studied Clough closely in recent years have different theories about how he and Taylor go about their job.

"We don't rule by fear," he says. "We're a democratic club, but you have to draw the line somewhere. Ask 16 different players what they want for dinner and you end up with 16 different dishes. It's rubbish to say we rule by fear, though. I'm paid to manage and I manage the way I think.

"You have to have the right judgment to get the right players and handle them properly. I've found that when things have gone wrong and I've listened to other poeple's opinions it's been a disaster. I won't let myself be influenced now. The more you listen to people the more you get off course.

"If my team plays badly we thrash it out in the dressing-room straight away, there and then. I do more talking than working. We once stayed in the dressing-room for an hour and a half after a defeat. It worked, though.

"I've been accused of being a bad loser and I am. What's a good loser? I don't know anyone in football who's a good loser.

"Ambitions? Yes, I've still got ambitions. I want to keep winning the Championship. The European Cup and domestic Cups are nice, but the Championship is the real thing. And I've won it twice with two small clubs . . ."

Brian Clough shares a hot cuppa with his partner and long-time friend, Peter Taylor (left).

Trevor wasn't just born to be a footballer. He was born to become a great one. Even as a small, under-sized lad at Pennycross Primary School he stood out as a "natural" with all the required talents. His local club, Plymouth Argyle, hoped to sign him, but were beaten by Birmingham City, one of the top clubs attracted by his performances for Plymouth in the English School's trophy . . .

. . .What a sensation he made when, on his first outing with the senior Blues' side, at the age of 16, he scored all their goals in a 4—0 home thrashing of Bolton! Since then, he's hit the headlines all over the World, including the U.S.A. where he has starred for Detroit Express (right).

Story of a star
TREVOR FRANCIS
FROM BOY WONDER TO SUPERMAN

One of his regrets is that he was never picked to play for England Schoolboys, but he's more than made up for that omission with tremendous displays for his country's other sides. He helped the Youth team win the Little World Cup in May, 1971, and again the following year.

Trevor has been on the mark with his distinctive goalgetting on many memorable occasions for the England Full side. (Left) He celebrates scoring England's second goal in their 5—0 win over Luxembourg at Wembley in March, 1977. (Above) Just over two years later, Trevor put on another five star performance, scoring two goals against Northern Ireland in Belfast, to help take England to a thrilling 5—1 victory.

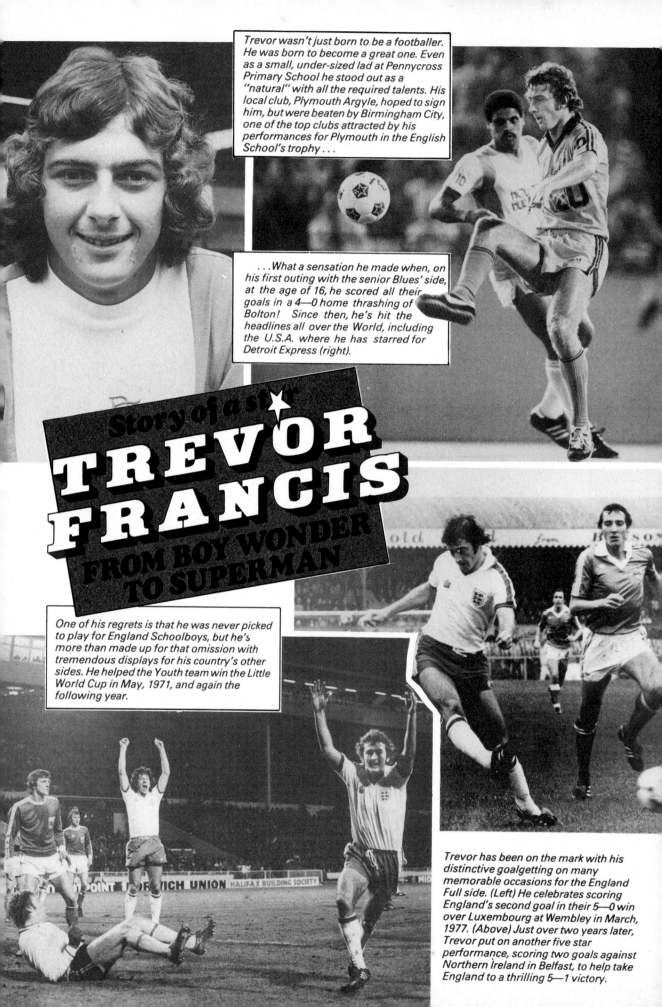

It's not been glory all the way for Trevor. He's touched the heights and known the agony of failure. Above he heads the goal that brought the European Cup to Forest in 1979. Below he attracts the attention of two Wolves players in 1980 when Forest lost 1—0 in the League Cup Final.

Probably the most significant milestone in an event-packed career was signing for Nottingham Forest in February, 1979. Here he poses with manager Brian Clough and assistant Peter Taylor to put the seal on a transfer that made him the first million pound player in Britain.

That defeat was followed by an even more shattering experience. A severe Achilles Tendon injury required surgery. For two months his leg was in plaster. Then came a slow, tortuous return to fitness, helped by his wife Helen. After seven and a half months on the sidelines he dispelled any doubts about whether he could regain his old form by scoring a comeback goal against Sunderland in a 3—1 win at the City Ground.

Willie Young has scored his share of vital goals during his career with Aberdeen, Spurs and Arsenal. Mainly from set-pieces or corners, where his height makes him almost unbeatable in the air.

But you can understand his disappointment when, in one game against Crystal Palace, he had a goal disallowed . . .it was an acrobatic overhead kick, which the referee ruled was dangerous kicking.

"Denis Law would have had dozens of his goals disallowed if that were the case," said a disgruntled Young. Yet there have been far more ups than downs for the likeable Scot, who more than makes up for what he lacks in natural ability by the sort of commitment and will-to-win that makes him a hero of the North Bank.

"Our competitive attitude is one of the main reasons why we've done so well," he says. "Don Howe must take much of the credit. He's a real driving force who never stops geeing us up. In training, during a match . . .wherever . . .Don is always on at us."

Arsenal have made Wembley their second home in recent years and while they haven't always been successful in the F.A. Cup, or the Cup-Winners' Cup, as Willie says: "I wouldn't have missed the experience for the world."

It's a long way from his early days back in Scotland where, believe it or not, he was a striker. "I used to play with kids older than myself and so was usually one of the smallest. At school our game was rugby, which I hated. I couldn't wait for weekend to arrive when I could play soccer.

"When I was 14 or 15 I suddenly started to grow very quickly and I was moved back into defence."

It was then that he caught the eye of an Aberdeen scout and he joined The Dons in 1968.

"I was a bit nervous at the trials. I could feel the adrenalin going. I just gave 100 per cent and Aberdeen signed me on. The attitude of some of the others was completely wrong, trying to be flash and impress in the wrong way."

Young quickly established himself in the Aberdeen team but like so many Scots, was eager to come over the border and try his luck in the English League.

A few clubs were interested in him. Spurs won the race for his signature in 1975, for £125,000.

He remembers: "The facilities were out of this world. They had their own training ground, everything was laid on, first-class hotels for away trips — a different cry from lunch on a train travelling to Glasgow or Edinburgh."

It was Terry Neill who signed Young, but things turned sour when the Irishman left for Arsenal.

"Keith Burkinshaw wanted me to play in a different way. He wanted me to do

more of a man-marking job, but I preferred to stay in the middle of defence.

"I felt that by leaving the centre I was leaving a huge gap. When the chance came to rejoin Terry at Arsenal I jumped at it."

You don't have to be a soccer genius to know that moving from Spurs to Arsenal isn't easy for a player. Two North London clubs with a strong rivalry.

"I had to win over the Arsenal fans," Willie concedes. "Terry paid only £80,000 for me, so I suppose people thought I couldn't be much good.

"In my first game we lost 4—1 to Ipswich and I gave away a penalty. Not the best of starts. A few weeks later we played Spurs and I cut my head badly. No way was I coming off. I had a few stitches inserted and carried on. I think the Arsenal fans appreciated that and since then we've had a great relationship."

Willie admits that playing alongside Republic of Ireland defender David O'Leary has been a big help to him. "He must be the most complete defender in Europe, mustn't he?" says Young. It's more of a statement than a question.

On the other hand, the Arsenal defence without Big Willie wouldn't be quite the same.

Cut head made Willie a hero

A SUPER SMITH

The oldest individual goalscoring record among Football League clubs was created 60 years ago by Joe Smith when he scored 38 First Division goals for Bolton Wanderers in season 1920-21. When you recall the hard-shooting forwards that have worn this club's colours since Joe Smith set that record it is amazing it has lasted so long.

Also surprising is the fact that Joe Smith was an inside-forward rather than a centre-forward, and in 1920-21, when most of the top scorers were centre-forwards, he played regularly at inside-left.

Under the old formation Joe Smith had the advantage of a remarkable partnership with his outside-left, Ted Vizard, probably the cleverest left-winger in the game at that time.

Joe Smith made 450 League appearances for Bolton 1908—1927, scoring 254 goals. He helped them win the F.A. Cup twice (1923 and 1926) and was manager of Blackpool when, by coincidence, they beat his old club in the 1953 Final. He had one of the hardest shots in the game.

Bolton's Joe Smith (above), holder of the oldest individual goalscoring record.

SEVEN-GOAL TED

They say that one man doesn't make a team but in 1936-37 Mansfield Town had a player who scored over 90 per cent of their goals — a record proportion of a team's goals claimed by one man. That player was centre-forward, Ted Harston, a Yorkshireman from Barnsley who had been floating around the League without too much success as a scorer before Mansfield Town secured his transfer from Bristol City in October 1935.

In his first League game for Mansfield (away to Southport) Harston scored all his side's goals in a 3—3 draw and ended his first season as top scorer with 26 goals in 29 games.

It was in the next season that he really hit the headlines, for after getting a hat-trick in the second game (at Rochdale) he scored five at home to the same opposition. In addition to a hat-trick against Halifax (home) and four against Hull City (home), he got five at home to Port Vale and seven in an 8—2 victory over Hartlepool. At the end of the season he had created a record for Division III(N) with 55 goals in 41 games. He also scored two in the F.A. Cup during this campaign in which Mansfield's next highest scorer was Arthur Atkinson with 10 goals.

TWO GAMES — TEN GOALS

We are constantly reading about famous goalscorers of the past but have you heard about Harry Brooks? Probably not, yet he played in the same team as some of England's finest internationals, men like Tommy Lawton, Cliff Britton, Wilf Copping, Arthur Cunliffe, Jimmy Hagan, Frank Swift, Stan Cullis and Joe Mercer.

The answer to this conundrum is that Harry Brooks was an Aldershot centre-forward signed by them from Doncaster Rovers just before the outbreak of World War II, and being a big Army centre all those famous players "guested" for Aldershot while they were in the Service in war-time games.

As for Harry's greatest goalscoring feat — he scored five goals in each of two consecutive F.A. Cup-ties for Aldershot during 1945-46, the only season in which this competition was fought on a two-leg home and away basis. Harry scored five when Reading were beaten 7—3 in a First Round (second-leg) tie, and another five in the first-leg of the next Round when Aldershot beat Newport (Isle of Wight) 7—0.

UNFAIR TO JIMMY

Blackpool's centre-forward for their F.A. Cup run through to the Final of 1948 was Jimmy McIntosh, a big Scot who had been brought up in Manchester and signed from Droylesden. Imagine his disappointment when after helping them reach Wembley he was dropped for the big game. Manager Joe Smith believed that inside-right Stan Mortensen's greater speed would be needed in the middle to beat Allen Chilton the Manchester United centre-half, and he also brought in Alec Munro at inside-right.

Blackpool were beaten 4—2 in that Final and as if to rub it in, only a week later in a First Division game at Preston, Jimmy McIntosh scored five goals in a 7—0 victory, thus equalling Blackpool's individual scoring record created by famous centre-forward, Jimmy Hampson, nearly 20 years earlier.

Blackpool's Jimmy McIntosh lost his place in the 1948 F.A. Cup Final to Stan Mortensen (above).

LONG SHOTS

Mention of Stan Mortensen brings back memories of many goalscoring feats by one of the most dashing strikers of the post-war era. Morty still holds an F.A. Cup record through having scored at least once in each of 12 consecutive Rounds (not every game). That run began with the Third Round of 1945-46 and ended in the Third Round of 1949-50. During that spell he also scored in nine consecutive F.A. Cup games.

There have been many great long distance scoring shots, but among those headed from the greatest distance was one by Aston Villa full-back, Peter Aldis, against Sunderland in the First Division, September 1st, 1952. It was reckoned to have been scored from 35 yards.

PUT 'EM BACK

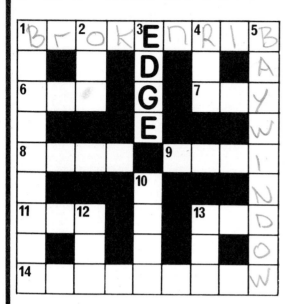

1 B	R	2 O	K	3 E	N	4 R	I	5 B

(Crossword grid — visible entries: 1 across BROKEN...RIB, 3 down EDGE, 5 down BAY-WINDOW)

There are no clues to this crossword with a soccer flavour — only the answers arranged alphabetically. Your task is to replace them all correctly, and you are given a one-word start.

Bay-window
Blackburn
Broken-rib
Due
Edge
Elm
Hull
Idol
Lad
Lou
Out
Row
WBA
Wimbledon
Yet
York

SEEK-A-STAR

Select just one letter from each row in the frame so as to spell out the name of a celebrated soccer personality. As a guide, the first one, KENNY SANSOM, has been indicated for you.

K	D	P	S	B	J	A	J	R	K
L	E	A	A	O	R	O	A	E	A
V	A	T	I	H	E	M	V	Y	N
A	I	N	J	C	N	I	M	N	C
D	E	Y	K	N	O	H	N	Y	L
N	W	T	S	E	O	R	E	K	N
A	N	L	N	A	E	M	R	A	E
I	L	N	T	E	N	I	L	E	L
N	E	B	N	S	G	S	G	S	I
N	D	C	G	A	O	A	O	O	O
M	N	Y	E	N	N	T	S	N	S

...AND TRACE A TEAM

Start at the top left-hand corner of this frame and, moving onto adjacent horizontal or vertical squares, trace out the names of 35 celebrated soccer clubs, marking off each square as you use it. As a guide, CHELSEA is indicated for you.

A	R	S	E	D	S	C	A	M	W	R	E	X	C	K	W	A	T	F	O
E	H	C	N	E	V	O	H	E	C	M	A	H	O	M	A	H	D	L	R
L	S	L	A	E	E	N	G	L	L	M	A	R	N	F	U	I	A	O	D
A	E	T	O	L	N	I	I	T	I	A	C	M	A	H	L	N	N	E	X
L	N	S	K	E	T	M	C	S	K	M	E	H	I	B	E	R	A	E	E
I	O	E	D	Y	R	R	M	R	R	B	E	O	M	G	N	I	D	R	T
V	T	R	B	Y	B	I	O	E	I	D	D	T	E	L	L	D	U	R	E
E	U	L	L	N	D	T	R	G	N	G	N	H	W	Y	L	C	M	B	A
R	P	O	O	E	N	O	B	E	A	E	U	E	R	D	E	N	O	T	R
T	S	A	C	W	A	N	A	R	R	B	D	Y	E	A	B	I	N	D	O
L	N	D	E	R	L	E	E	D	A	U	R	N	L	N	S	W	R	T	N
E	U	S	R	E	T	N	R	D	E	S	N	A	G	K	Y	B	A	E	R
L	E	I	C	E	S	C	A	I	F	F	S	W	R	I	M	S	N	M	E

Find your favourites

First give a surname to the forenames listed in the frame on left, the bracketed number indicating how many letters there are in each. Then transfer your attention to the grid on right, in which all your answers are spelt out TWICE in straight lines, horizontally, vertically or diagonally and forwards or backwards. As a guide, the first one, MILLS, is indicated and traced on the grid. The rest should keep you busy for a while.

#	Forename	Surname
1	MICK (5)	MILLS
2	Ray (7)	Wilkins
3	Trevor (8)	Brooking
4	Frank (7)	Stapelton
5	Stuart (7)	Pearson
6	Lou (6)	Macrary
7	Graham (3)	R
8	Brian (6)	
9	Joe (4)	
10	Kevin (7)	Keegan
11	John (4)	
12	Allan (6)	
13	Eddie (4)	Gray
14	Derek (7)	
15	Billy (6)	
16	Kenny (6)	Keegan
17	Phil (4)	Neal
18	Jimmy (4)	
19	Ian (4)	
20	Gary (6)	Lineker

```
B I W G N I K O O R B
E M O U L D R A W D L
A X I R O E M A S V Y
T R E L T I R A Y D D
T U T N L D N O E S E
I S U L C S G N L G N
E H S R O L N R I R N
N I U M E E I W A A E
A R T N K X K T B Y K
L A J T T M O A T E C
R C K I A E O D Y L E
A A L C L E R A A I E
P M A N H A B K R A W
L R E D P H M V G B P
I A N M E S U P E E S
T H A O A U E G A E K
T L L S R R H R H R N
L E R N S R S G A E D
E S A A O O U W A S S
U A P S N H R L A E N
M C F E S A C O E K C
```

WEE WORDS WANTED

Solve the "down" clues, and 19 across should spell out the name of a Scottish team.

1 Bashful
2 Insane
3 Demon
4 Large
5 Aged
6 Consumed
7 Crib
8 Finish
9 Rodent
10 Frozen
11 Evil
12 Uneven
13 Wager
14 Girl's name
15 Gratuity
16 Pilot
17 Feline
18 Cunning

1	2	3	4	5	6	7	8	9	10	11	12	13	14	15	16	17	18
19																	

Answers on page 30.

VOICE OF THE VIKINGS

Norwegian soccer club Viking Stavanger had just chalked up another victory and a jubilant group of their supporters were bawdily swaying their way homewards, well fortified with warming wine or whisky. Their singing, outside his house, annoyed 68-year-old Olaf Lindholm, who was trying to listen to his radio. When his protests were drowned by their jeers, he made more forcible overtures, by emptying white paint over their heads from an upstairs window. The whiter-than-white revellers were seen off by police, called to intervene when they tried to break down Olaf's door and deal with him.

KICKING OFF WISELY

East German forward Emil Gerhardt landed heavily on the sodden Dresden pitch and the referee immediately blew for a penalty. But Emil rushed towards him, assured him that he had fallen and not been tripped by the opposing defender. The ref altered his decision and play was resumed. Interviewed after the game, Emil explained: "I'm marrying that player's sister, Hildegarde, next Saturday. I didn't want to get off on the wrong foot with the family, did I?"

WHACKO, WACKER

Austrian soccer team Wacker Vienna had scored three times, and each time enthusiastic supporter Fraulein Ilse Riedmann had flung her arms around the men nearest her in the crowd and kissed them in jubilation. After the game, no fewer than six of them wanted to date her. She told them all: "See me here at our next home fixture, and I'll go out with the one who can successfully predict the result of the game." Wacker Vienna won that match 2—0, and the happy prophet was bakery worker Luther Bichel, aged 37 and just 18 years older than Ilse. But she kept her word, and the date proved so successful that the pair were married within weeks.

A REAL HE-MAN

His team, Real Madrid, were a goal down, and ardent supporter Alfonso Carlevera was dejected. When a mate jokingly told him that he looked as if he had the devil on his back, he countered: "If only we could beat this lot, I wouldn't mind having you and the devil on my back. I'd carry you all the way home." Then the Real Madrid XI showed the stuff they were made of and scored three goals without any rejoinder from their visitors. True to his word, Alfonso, who weighs just 10st 5lbs, carried his friend, 12½stone Manuelo Avila, all the way home, a matter of 800 metres, without pause for rest or refreshment.

BAREFACED CHEEK

A visiting forward seemed to have been brought down in the penalty area, but A.C.Milan supporter Vittorio Manini yelled to all and sundry that the man had taken a dive. But from the spot, the player scored a goal, which left Vittorio fuming. Seconds later, play reached the area in front of where Vittorio was seated. He scrambled over fencing onto the pitch, dived at the player's legs and pulled down his shorts. As the man tried to cover his confusion, Vittorio slapped his bottom hard — twice, before linesmen escorted him from the pitch and into the arms of the law. Later, he was fined.

VARCONI IN THE VAT

Portuguese wine bottler Rodriguez Varconi was thrilled when his idols, Benfica, agreed to give him a test "in the net". He had played for his school and his wine exporting firm as a goalkeeper and felt that he was good enough to play for a real team with international repute. However, disaster befell him on the eve of the big day, when he was to receive his trial. He celebrated not wisely but well and his unsteady legs could not carry so much wine. He toppled into a vat of port-type wine, and would have drowned but for the timely arrival of a colleague. Hundreds of gallons of wine were condemned as being unfit for consumption, following his reluctant bath, and Rodriguez was sacked. Nor did Benfica any longer want to know anything about a player of such intemperate habits.

HOT STUFF FROM SPURS

Away fixtures by Tottenham Hotspur don't leave Mrs Alice Ridley cold — quite the reverse in fact. With her husband and two sons, she motored to Birmingham to watch her idols play at St Andrews and, during the game, started to pour hot coffee from her vacuum flask for a warming drink. Suddenly, whoosh! The ball was booted straight into her lap, causing her to spill the coffee over her new blue raincoat, and raise a couple of burn blisters on her wrist. Just two weeks later, watching her team playing Liverpool at Anfield Road, the same thing happened — but this time the coffee was spilled into her husband's lap. He announced: "In future, we'll take a metal hip flask of whisky instead. Nobody, not even the Spurs, dare spill my whisky."

It's a funny old world

SHOOT columnist Gordon McQueen takes time off from Manchester United to play a round at the Northenden Golf Club.

Players have a swinging time...

WITH ANOTHER KIND OF CLUB

West Brom stars past and present enjoy the calm of the golf course . . . Bobby Hope, John Trewick (now Newcastle) and John Wile.

Derby County striker Dave Swindlehurst deep in thought as he ponders over which club to choose.

Late-starter Devonshire makes up for lost time

By the age of 19 most would-be international stars have had a taste of first-team football. Three or four years experience of being with a professional club. The right coaching...the right environment for a soccer star.

At 19 Alan Devonshire was a fork-lift truck operator playing for Southall in the Isthmian League. He'd been turned down by one or two League clubs and had virtually resigned himself to being a part-time player.

Then West Ham became aware of the raw midfielder whose pace was outstanding, even at a lower level. They watched him and saw the sort of skill that proper coaching could turn from potential to reality. And when it comes to skill, a player couldn't ask for a better club than West Ham to fulfill his ambitions:

"There isn't a player in the League who appreciates being a professional more than I do," says Alan. "Because I arrived late I probably have a different outlook to those who joined clubs straight from school.

"I never gave up hope of making the grade, but when you reach the age of 19 and you haven't been signed...well, you have to consider an alternative career."

Devonshire needed little or no time to adapt to the demands of being a full-timer. "The first couple of weeks of training was murder. I went home every day with my body aching. I soon became used to it, though.

"Playing in the Isthmian League toughened me up. Some of the players you come up against at that level don't worry about their opponents' welfare. Football isn't their living. I'm not saying the pro game is perfect, but I've found more respect at this level than at non-League.

"Professionals get stuck in. Let's say there isn't nearly the amount of deliberately bad tackling you find outside the Football League. Pros know that by injuring an opponent they're virtually taking away his livelihood."

As one of the most skilful players in the country Devonshire naturally attracts the sort of tackles soccer can do without. Luckily he is blessed with such natural speed and balance that he can ride most tackles with ease.

"I've studied Trevor Brooking closely. He's similar to me in that he likes to run at defences with the ball. I was never coached or taught tactics until I joined Southall. Until then I'd done my own thing.

"Although I'm basically an attacking player I realise I have to do my share of grafting when we haven't got the ball."

'Unbelievable'

Over the course of a season, a neutral fan would arguably see more exciting games following West Ham than any other club. Upton Park, with the fans almost on the touchline, is ready-made for Cup-tie atmosphere, while the emphasis at the club, under Ron Greenwood and carried on by John Lyall, has always been on attack.

Last season saw the emergence of Geoff Pike a class midfielder, and with Patsy Holland and teenager Paul Allen, the West Ham midfield was always packed with the good things in football.

Devonshire won England B honours and then followed Trevor 'Hadleigh' Brooking into the full England team.

"Playing in West Ham's first team was a big enough honour, but to win an F.A. Cup medal and a full England cap in the same year was unbelievable. I was rubbing shoulders with household names...players I'd watched on T.V."

Alan Devonshire, the former fork-lift truck driver, has certainly come up in the world...and is set to go even higher.

It isn't often Brian Clough makes mistakes, let alone admits to one. But even Cloughie had to eat a small portion of humble pie as far as Archie Gemmill was concerned.

Clough had signed the Scottish midfielder twice, for Derby and then Nottingham Forest. Gemmill won Championship medals with both clubs.

When Forest won the first of their two European Cups in 1979 Gemmill didn't play. As Forest won, beating Malmö 1—0, perhaps Clough's team selection was justified.

It was obviously the beginning of the end and soon afterwards Gemmill was on his way from the City Ground to Birmingham City, for a mere £150,000. Ironically, Blues can say Gemmill didn't really cost them anything as they

Argentina, and when he wasn't picked by Ally MacLeod for the opening game against Peru he virtually wrote himself off.

Then, after losing to Peru and only drawing against Iran, Gemmill was chosen to face Holland and responded by scoring the goal of the tournament, a brilliant solo effort when he beat two defenders and the goalkeeper before slotting the ball home.

Then Jock Stein took over and saw the veteran midfielder as the man to give Scotland a kiss of life.

"This was one of the highlights of my career, being recalled as skipper. I like to think I've managed to combine both jobs successfully.

"I've never thought I had anything to prove to Brian Clough or anyone."

'I HAD NOTHING TO PROVE' —Archie Gemmill

still had money left over from the £1 million they'd received the previous year for Trevor Francis!

Some thought Archie was past his best. Presumably Clough did. A few months later the Forest manager was big enough to admit he sold Archie too soon; that the player could still have done a job for Forest.

Birmingham were delighted with Clough's boob. Blues boss Jim Smith immediately made Gemmill team captain as Birmingham started a campaign that was to see them win promotion back to Division One.

Scotland manager Jock Stein also handed Archie the captaincy of his country. For someone supposedly past his best Gemmill wasn't doing too badly. Nor has he done too badly since!

He inspired Blues to promotion and helped them establish themselves in the First Division. Gemmill's enthusiasm and leadership were just what the St. Andrews club needed, although Gemmill, typically, is keen to play down his contribution.

"Birmingham have succeeded because we have a lot of good players. The youngsters have gained in experience and confidence. Many had tasted relegation and this knocked them back a bit. Once the side started to win everything was different.

"I realise Birmingham signed me for my experience and to help them win promotion. I'm delighted I played my part, but I'm only one player and football isn't a one-man game."

Gemmill admits he thought his Scotland career was over during the 1978 World Cup Finals. He was taken to

Did Nottingham Forest boss Brian Clough (below) regret allowing Archie to leave for Birmingham City?

Old Firm action as Rangers' Colin McAdam outjumps Celtic's Danny McGrain.

MICKEY THOMAS
Manchester United

APPEARANCE RECORDS

QUICK CHANGE

In season 1937-38 Jack Beattie, a Scottish inside or centre-forward, appeared for three different clubs in the First Division in the space of 64 days. He began the season with Birmingham and last played for them on December 11th. Early in January he was transferred to Huddersfield Town and made three appearances for them before moving on to Grimsby Town where he made his debut on February 12th.

48 LEAGUE OUTINGS IN ONE SEASON

The famous Scottish international inside-forward, Tommy Walker, made 48 League appearances in season 1946-47! The first nine of these were in the Scottish League with his original club, Heart of Midlothian, but in September 1946 Chelsea secured the transfer of this talented footballer at a bargain price, and before the season had ended he had added 39 Football League appearances to his total.

DIFFICULT POSITION

The position which has seen most changes in the England team is inside-right. No player has ever made more than seven consecutive appearances in the No. 10 position, but four have made that number — Raich Carter (1946-47), Stan Mortensen (1947-48), Jimmy Greaves (1962) (below) and Steve Coppell (1979-79).

BILLY BEST

The record run of consecutive appearances in any position for England is 46 at centre-half by Billy Wright (1954-59). The former Wolves star also holds the England record for the right-half position with a run of 24 appearances (1951-54).

CUP-TIED

Although not a record it is noteworthy that during his 12 seasons with Blackpool goalkeeper George Farm never missed a single F.A. Cup tie. Joining Blackpool from Hibernian in 1948 he played in 47 consecutive Cup ties to February 1960 when he returned to Scotland and joined Queen of the South. From his debut for Blackpool in September 1948 he had enjoyed a run of 188 consecutive League and Cup games.

EMLYN'S RUN

The record run of consecutive F.A. Cup appearances is 63 by Emlyn Hughes (above) with Blackpool and Liverpool. This run began in the Third Round with Blackpool in 1966-67 when they were beaten by Birmingham City shortly before his transfer to Liverpool. In the following season Emlyn commenced a run of 62 F.A. Cup ties with the Reds, ending with the Semi-Final replay against Manchester United in 1978-79.

SEVEN IN FOUR

Goalkeeper John Hope appeared in all four Divisions of the Football League in the course of only seven consecutive League games. He was with Darlington in 1966-67 playing in Division Three. The following season they were relegated to Division Four. In 1968, Hope moved to Newcastle and played one game in the First Division before transferring to Sheffield United and appearing for them in the Second Division in 1970-71.

HARD WORKER

On Goose Fair Saturday, October 6th 1888, the Notts County club put on an extra game at Trent Bridge, playing Eckington in the First Qualifying Round of the F.A. Cup before meeting Blackburn Rovers in the Football League. As with many League clubs at that time Notts fielded their reserves in the F.A. Cup tie, but one player, full-back B.F. Warburton, appeared for Notts in both games, helping them beat the Derbyshire side 4—1 in the Cup and draw with Blackburn 3—3 in the League. All in the space of about 3½ hours.

WAR HERO

One of the stars of Welsh football between the two World Wars as well as a hero in World War I, where he won the Military Medal and the Belgian Croix de Guerre, was Stanley Davies. In 18 appearances for Wales he was selected for six different positions — centre-forward (6), inside-left (4), inside-right (3), outside-right (2), right-half (2), and left-half (1). He also played full-back in an emergency and at Wrexham in February 1922, when playing at outside-right, he got his side's second goal against Scotland before the visitors reduced the arrears, but when the Welsh goalkeeper was injured with 20 minutes left for play Stan went in goal and prevented the Scots from getting an equaliser.

UNLUCKY NICK

Bill Nicholson, who spent the whole of his professional career with Tottenham Hotspur, including 16 years as Manager, obliged with a goal when making his debut for England (against Portugal at Goodison Park in May 1951) yet he never appeared for England again. Bill was unlucky enough to be competing with Billy Wright for the right-half position.

ARSENAL AMATEURS

The F.A. no longer recognises amateurs (unpaid players) as such, but before the distinction between amateurs and professionals was erased in 1974 the greatest number of true amateurs to appear in a Football League side since World War Two was three. Surprisingly enough this was in a First Division game when Bernard Joy (centre-half), Albert Gudmundsson (inside-right), and Dr. Kevin O'Flanagan (outside-left), played for Arsenal against Stoke at Highbury, October 19th, 1946. Arsenal won 1—0 with Dr. O'Flanagan getting the winner. Gudmundsson was an Icelander.

ALAN BRAZIL – THE OTHER PELE

If there's a youngster somewhere called Kevin Keegan or Bobby Moore imagine what problems he'll face if he ever makes the grade as a professional.

Alan Brazil, the Ipswich and Scotland striker, feels under no pressure at all with his nickname, even though it's the name of the most famous and gifted player the world has ever produced: Pele.

Naturally it's all tongue-in-cheek and with a surname like Brazil it was inevitable that the Scot would end up being likened to the former famous South American star.

If Alan is now almost as well-known, it's been a hard road to the top. Born in the Scottish soccer capital of Glasgow, he first came to notice playing for Celtic Boys Club, where he was a regular goalscorer.

Surprisingly the scouts of Celtic and Rangers hesitated, but the Ipswich representative saw something in the raw talent of the free-scoring teenager and invited him down to Portman Road for a trial.

Ipswich decided Brazil was good enough and he became an apprentice in 1976. He waited in the junior team for a couple of years until he was promoted to the reserves.

"It may sound stange," he says, "but making my debut for the reserves was a big moment for me. It was quite a step up from the youth team and I was delighted to progress in such a way.

"I'd been at the club for a while and was beginning to wonder if I'd ever be upgraded. Then I set my thoughts on a first-team spot."

Despite being a regular scorer in the reserves, Brazil had few opportunities in the League side. His frustration was broken by the chance to play in America during the summer of 1978.

"Detroit Express wanted me on loan. The main attraction was that I'd be playing alongside Trevor Francis, which I thought could only improve my game.

"I did quite well over there and when I came back I was more confident. Not only that, playing on Astroturf had helped my ball control and speed off the mark.

"I found I could handle the pace of the First Division easier after the 'working holiday'. The following season I played in around half of Ipswich's games, which proved to me how much I'd progressed."

Since then Brazil has become an established First Division star, with Ipswich able to challenge the big city clubs for dominance.

His partnership up front with Paul Mariner has become one of the deadliest in Division One. And with little Eric Gates always in support, Town aren't very often goal-less after 90 minutes.

"We have the right blend of youth and experience, with some useful people like Kevin Beattie ready to step in. I believe this side can stay at the top for a long time.

"From a personal point of view I'd like to establish myself in the Scotland team. I made my debut on our summer tour in 1980 when I came on as sub against Hungary and Poland.

"I know there are a lot of good strikers for Jock Stein to choose from, such as Andy Gray and Kenny Dalglish, but I'll be doing my best to ensure I stay in the reckoning."

Perhaps soon we'll hear "Pele" chanted from the Hampden Park terraces!

Because of his surname, the Ipswich star (left) has been likened to the fabulous Brazilian goalscorer (inset).

ANOTHER CRACKER

Kenny Dalglish would be delighted to see a Scottish club win the European Cup . . .as long as it wasn't at Liverpool's expense! Dalglish was just an up-and-coming youngster when Celtic won the European Cup in 1967. Since then, of course, the player with the record number of caps for Scotland has gone on to win European Cup glory with Liverpool. Last season the Champions of England were paired with Aberdeen,

FROM KENNY...

the pride of Scotland. Surprisingly there have been few such England/Scotland clashes in Europe. Liverpool did the double over The Dons, winning at both Pittodrie and Anfield. One of the highlights of the two tremendous ties was this superbly headed goal by Kenny, who couldn't hide his delight, even if the opposition DID include some of his international team-mates!

In these days when hundreds of thousands of fans can watch their teams from the comfort of huge grandstands with all modern facilities do you ever wonder what conditions were like in years gone by?

There are few of the big clubs of today who began life at their present headquarters. Take Arsenal as an example. They began way back in 1886 under the title of Royal Arsenal because most of their players and spectators worked at Woolwich Arsenal making Naval guns. Their first pitch was a field surrounded by hedges to survive.

So they took over the disused playing field of a school in North London and moved lock, stock and barrel to start again! It worked. Today Arsenal's home at Highbury is one of the finest grounds in the country.

Only a short bus ride from Highbury is White Hart Lane, home of Spurs. But like Arsenal, Spurs played their early games on a muddy marsh with the consent of the landowner. After each game they upended their goalposts — made by the father of one of the lads — and left them in the care of the local home of their own. So they took over the kitchen garden of a big mansion known as Aston Hall and turned it into the now famous Villa Park ground.

Wolves had a similar rise to glory after starting as a humble youth club, St. Lukes, attached to the local church. Their first ground was a park pitch but as they progressed after amalgamating with the Wanderers, a local cricket club, they took over the title of Wolverhampton Wanderers and moved to another ground. Then in 1889, after being elected to the Football League, they took over a park,

ARMY WAGONS -
ARSENAL'S GRANDSTAND

and trees. Their captain acted as gatekeeper to collect the SIXPENNY entrance fees of the few fans interested. Their first "grandstand" was a couple of Army wagons, loaned by the Royal Artillery stationed at Woolwich.

In 1893, however, after two changes of grounds, The Gunners joined the Football League and began to develop the Manor Ground not far from their first "field of play". It wasn't very successful. The fans were few and far between and by 1913, even though they were then in the First Division, Woolwich Arsenal as they were still known, faced bankruptcy. Drastic measures were needed if the club was

stationmaster. But after a couple of seasons they managed to rent a private ground in the local park and received permission to charge for admission. Their first games amounted to the sum of 17 shillings!

In 1898, then a professional club in the Southern League, they bought up what had been a market garden at the rear of the White Hart public house in the Tottenham High Road. With the help of local fans the new headquarters of Tottenham Hotspur became reality and today are a famous ground.

Aston Villa are another club whose first "ground" was a pitch in local parkland with haystacks behind one of the goals and a row of trees marking a touchline. After two seasons they rented a piece of ground at nearby Perry Barr, but a few years later when they were elected to the Football League they decided they needed a

White City, where Q.P.R. played before moving to Loftus Road. (Below): The original Crystal Palace ground, scene of F.A. Cup Finals between 1895 and 1914.

Molineux, with a boating lake, fountains, etc.

Manchester City began their career in 1894, when they took over from Ardwick F.C. who went broke. Their ground in those days was at Hyde Road. But City's progress attracted such big crowds that the ground was far too small. A new ground was needed so City bought up a disused refuse tip at Maine Road. It is now one of the finest grounds in the League.

Bolton Wanderers had several grounds during their early days — including the one at Pike's Lane which was little better than a mudheap during the winter. They set up home at their

Well, when the club began in 1884 they took over part of the old Derby racecourse and there they stayed until 1895.

Meanwhile, an American living in Derby had started a baseball club with a very well-appointed ground almost in the centre of the town. But the people of Derby showed little interest and within a few months the baseball club disbanded. It was a stroke of luck for Derby County who had been looking for a chance to leave the old Racecourse Ground, so they started afresh at the Baseball Ground.

Blackburn Rovers' first ground was part of a farm field which they rented

World War, however, they were forced to move, so they restarted at The Nest, the ground formerly used by the defunct Croydon Common club. They moved to their present ground Selhurst Park in 1925.

Fulham's early days were fraught with ground problems. In the short space of about a dozen years they had five different "homes". Each time they found a good pitch they were soon ousted by builders. One of their pitches was shared with a cricket and Rugby club. In 1806, however, they moved to a "wilderness" on the banks of the Thames once the gardens of Craven Cottage. There was so much work to be done on the site that they had to play all their "home" games on opponents' grounds.

Cardiff City, who began life in 1899 as Cardiff Riverside, had a number of grounds during their early years, but in 1910 when they adopted professionalism and changed their name to Cardiff City, they purchased some waste ground, formerly allotments that had become a weed-choked wilderness and rubbish dump, spent months clearing it and turning it into the very fine ground now known throughout football as Ninian Park.

Where many big clubs first kicked-off — and how they progressed to their present grounds

present headquarters in 1895 at Burnden Park, once a rubbish tip.

Few clubs had more grounds than West Bromwich Albion during their early years. Between 1879 and 1900 they had five different home grounds including the Dartmouth Cricket Club pitch and Stoney Lane — which they rented at £25 a year for 15 years, until their new ground was opened in 1901. That was The Hawthorns their present home.

West Ham — originally Thames Ironworks (their original players were mostly men who built battleships) — had their first ground at Hermit Road where the pitch was mostly loose cinders! Their next was a recreation ground at Canning Town, East London, but in 1904 they moved into their present home, the Boleyn Ground, so named because Anne Boleyn, one of Henry VIII's Queens, lived in a mansion which had stood at one corner of the ground.

You may have wondered why Derby County play at the Baseball Ground.

for a few shillings a match. In the middle of the field was a small cattle pond which on match days was bridged with planks and covered with turf. During one game — yes, it happened! — the planks gave way and a visiting player had to be dragged out of the muddy water! Rovers soon moved to another ground but in 1890 took over their present headquarters at Ewood Park.

Crystal Palace, formed in 1905 by workers at the huge entertainment centre in South-east London, had a ready-made ground — the excellent pitch on which Cup Finals were played between 1895 and 1914. After the First

Queens Park Rangers should have been called "Wanderers" because of their frequent moves from ground to ground during their early years. They first went to their present ground Loftus Road in 1917 but twice moved to White City, now a famous London sports stadium, before settling down at Loftus Road. Charlton Athletic also spent their early years switching from ground to ground, eventually taking over The Valley in 1920. However, gates dropped away and in 1922 they moved to nearby Catford where the only "grandstand" was a large tarpaulin stretched on scaffold poles! The experiment failed so back went Charlton to The Valley.

STAN CUMMINS
Sunderland

**DENNIS
MORTIMER**
Aston Villa

DOUBLE TROUBLE

See if you can identify these look-alikes . . .

A: (left) An English county is linked with this hard-hitting Hammer.

B: (below) Chelsea star with the name that sounds like a Greek island.

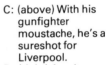

C: (above) With his gunfighter moustache, he's a sureshot for Liverpool.

D: (right) Another master marksman — from the North-East.

E: (left) "I'm running this show" says The Gunners' defender.

F: (above) A big smile from Steve -------- of Manchester City.

Answers: A: Alan Devonshire of West Ham. B: Peter Rhoades-Brown. C: David Johnson. D: David Hodgson of 'Boro. E: Kenny Sansom of Arsenal. F: McKenzie.

'I'M NO VETERAN'
insists St.Mirren's Jimmy Bone

ABERDEEN'S international defensive double-act of Willie Miller and Stuart Kennedy were left utterly aghast and helpless as a soccer whirlwind whipped past them.

That 'whirlwind' was St. Mirren attacker Jimmy Bone and it brought him one of the most outstanding goals in Scottish football last season in a rollicking 1—1 Premier League draw at Love Street.

Bone was in his own half when he collected the ball and simply took off with breathtaking acceleration in the direction of the Aberdeen goal. He shrugged off all around him as he tore into the penalty box and sent a rasping low shot wide of the despairing dive of goalkeeper Jim Leighton.

"Now maybe people will stop calling me a veteran," declared Jimmy after his lung-bursting run. "As soon as you get past 30 in this game people start calling you a geriatric. I think I've still got quite a bit to go to when I finally hang up my boots.

"I'll quit football when I think I am ready to make that decision. I won't be forced into anything. I don't rate myself as a veteran. Why, I'm just a youngster!"

Love Street manager Rikki McFarlane backs up his 32-year-old front-runner by saying: "He's easily one of the fittest men at the club. He's not quite ready to be put down just yet! I hope Jimmy Bone will be with St. Mirren for an awful long time to come.

"I've got to laugh whenever I read about Jimmy being a veteran. Do you know he is one of the swiftest players at this club, but he rarely gets the credit he undoubtedly deserves?

"People tend to think of him as being a bit slow. They should get out there on the park and try to keep up with him!"

Certainly Aberdeen's Willie Miller and Stuart Kennedy had no easy answer last season when Bone got into his stride before scoring that brilliant effort.

"St. Mirren rescued my career," says Bone. "I was with Arbroath when they came for me to give me another chance at the big time. I'll always be grateful to them for that opportunity.

"Don't get me wrong, though. I was happy with Arbroath. I put my game together with them after failing to hit it off with Celtic and that will always remain a disappointment in my career.

"I went to Parkhead full of hope, but things just didn't work out. Still, that's football. I'm delighted to be with St. Mirren and I think we are easily one of the most entertaining teams in Britain."

Bone started his career with Partick Thistle and, in fact, scored a goal in their astonishing 4—1 League Cup Final triumph over Celtic in 72. He then moved to Norwich and onto Sheffield United before returning to Scotland with Celtic.

He may have been around for a while, but pity the man who calls Jimmy Bone a veteran!

**KEVIN
KEEGAN
Southampton**

**ALEX
SABELLA
Leeds Utd.**

THE WEST HAM STORY

IF YOU enjoy watching good football week after week go along to Upton Park in London's East End — the home of West Ham United.

Fewer teams provide as much entertainment as The Hammers. Unfortunately their stylish football has often flattered to deceive, failing to bring them the number of expected honours.

John Lyall was aware of that even before he took over from Ron Greenwood in December, 1977, to become only the fifth manager in the club's history . . . a club born in 1900 out of the ashes of the bankrupt Thames Ironworks F.C.

In 1904, West Ham, then a struggling Southern League side, moved from the

The Cockney Kings have added steel to style

Memorial Grounds in Canning Town to their present Upton Park, the site of a cleared cabbage patch.

Among the players who joined West Ham in those very early days were Syd King and Charlie Paynter.

When his playing days were over King became West Ham's first manager and kept the job until 1931. He was succeeded by Paynter, who became a trainer when forced to retire through injury.

The Hammers remained a Southern League team until 1919, when they won election to the Second Division.

They soon established themselves in the Football League and in 1923 won promotion to the First Division.

That same year, with left-half Jack Tresadern and centre-forward Vic Watson — the scorer of a club record 306 goals — winning England caps, West Ham reached the F.A. Cup Final.

It was Wembley's Opening Day, and the largest crowd to gather for a football match in this country invaded the brand-new stadium.

An estimated 200,000 fans spilled over the terraces and on to the pitch. Few actually saw much of the action as West Ham went down 2—0 to Bolton Wanderers.

The club remained a good First Division side until 1932 when they

---

West Ham return to East London in triumph after beating Arsenal in the 1980 F.A. Cup Final.

were relegated, despite the presence of famous stars Ted Hufton in goal, winger Jimmy Ruffell and Len Goulden.

A 1—0 win over Blackburn Rovers at Wembley in a Wartime Cup Final was little consolation to a club that languished in the Second Division for 26 years until their return to the top flight in 1957-58.

Eight members of the side that won the Second Division Championship with 101 goals — goalkeeper Ernie Gregory, John Bond, Malcolm Allison, Noel Cantwell, Ken Brown, Eddie Lewis, Billy Lansdowne and Malcolm Musgrove — were later to spread the West Ham gospel as managers or coaches.

Also out of the Upton Park Academy came Dave Sexton, Frank O'Farrell, Andy Nelson, Jimmy Andrews, Phil Woosnam, Johnny Cartwright, Jimmy Bloomfield, Martin Peters, Geoff Hurst and John Lyall.

The man responsible for taking West Ham back to the First Division in 1958 was Ted Fenton who had succeeded Charlie Paynter in 1950.

But it wasn't until the arrival of Ron Greenwood in 1961 that West Ham really began to look like a club capable of winning trophies rather than simply taking part.

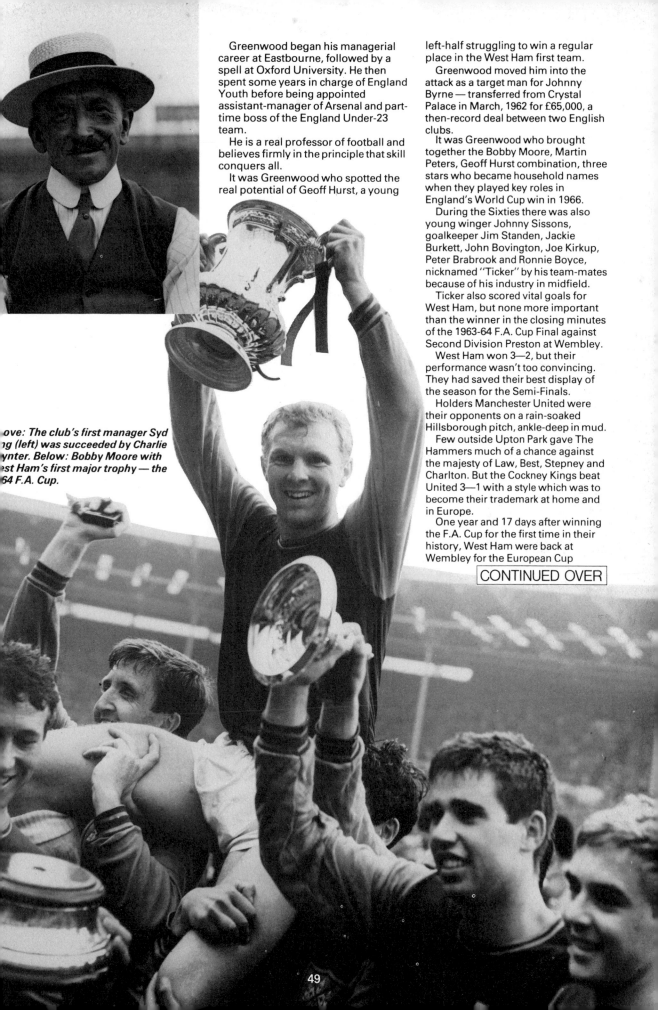

Greenwood began his managerial career at Eastbourne, followed by a spell at Oxford University. He then spent some years in charge of England Youth before being appointed assistant-manager of Arsenal and part-time boss of the England Under-23 team.

He is a real professor of football and believes firmly in the principle that skill conquers all.

It was Greenwood who spotted the real potential of Geoff Hurst, a young left-half struggling to win a regular place in the West Ham first team.

Greenwood moved him into the attack as a target man for Johnny Byrne — transferred from Crystal Palace in March, 1962 for £65,000, a then-record deal between two English clubs.

It was Greenwood who brought together the Bobby Moore, Martin Peters, Geoff Hurst combination, three stars who became household names when they played key roles in England's World Cup win in 1966.

During the Sixties there was also young winger Johnny Sissons, goalkeeper Jim Standen, Jackie Burkett, John Bovington, Joe Kirkup, Peter Brabrook and Ronnie Boyce, nicknamed "Ticker" by his team-mates because of his industry in midfield.

Ticker also scored vital goals for West Ham, but none more important than the winner in the closing minutes of the 1963-64 F.A. Cup Final against Second Division Preston at Wembley.

West Ham won 3—2, but their performance wasn't too convincing. They had saved their best display of the season for the Semi-Finals.

Holders Manchester United were their opponents on a rain-soaked Hillsborough pitch, ankle-deep in mud.

Few outside Upton Park gave The Hammers much of a chance against the majesty of Law, Best, Stepney and Charlton. But the Cockney Kings beat United 3—1 with a style which was to become their trademark at home and in Europe.

One year and 17 days after winning the F.A. Cup for the first time in their history, West Ham were back at Wembley for the European Cup

CONTINUED OVER

ove: The club's first manager Syd ng (left) was succeeded by Charlie ynter. Below: Bobby Moore with st Ham's first major trophy — the 64 F.A. Cup.

Winners' Cup Final against TSV Munich 1860.

Alan Sealey stole the glory by scoring the two goals that gave The Hammers a victory described as one of the all-time classic Finals.

West Ham seemed close to perfection, on the threshold of more glory. Upton Park fans had their sights on the Championship.

But apart from a League Cup Final appearance in 1966 when they were soundly thrashed over two-legs by West Brom, and eighth place in the First Division in 1968-69, The Hammers lost their way.

In March, 1970, Ron Greenwood reluctantly sold Martin Peters to Spurs for £200,000 plus £54,000-rated Jimmy Greaves.

The Greaves end of the deal was never a success and West Ham struggled to avoid relegation. "Bubbles", the popular theme song of the Upton Park faithful, had burst.

In 1971, Greenwood spent £500,000 in a desperate bid to restore West Ham to their peak of the middle Sixties.

Scottish international goalkeeper Bobby Ferguson came from Kilmarnock for £65,000; centre-back Tommy Taylor from Orient for £78,000; Peter Eustace from Sheffield Wednesday for £90,000 and Bryan "Pop" Robson from Newcastle for £120,000.

Of them all Pop Robson was the biggest hit at Upton Park, scoring over 100 goals for the club in the two spells he had with them.

Moore, Peters, Hurst, Robson and Ron Greenwood have all left the club, which now boasts a team more competitive, more efficient, better equipped for the modern game.

Behind the great Trevor Brooking and Alan Devonshire in midfield there is the steel hardness of Ray Stewart, a £400,000 signing from Dundee United, a scorer of vital penalties, among them the equaliser in the 1981 League Cup Final v. Liverpool at Wembley; the brilliance of giant goalkeeper Phil Parkes a record £500,000 buy from Q.P.R., and young centre-half Alvin Martin.

Up front there's the lethal finishing of David Cross (£180,000 from West Brom), and Paul Goddard (£800,000 from Q.P.R.). The unselfish running of long-serving Pat Holland and Geoff Pike. The potential of Paul Allen, Bobby Barnes and Nicky Morgan.

And of course, there's battling Billy Bonds, a swashbuckling skipper who made a tremendous contribution to West Ham's F.A. Cup victories of 1975 (v. Fulham) and 1980 (v. Arsenal) and their successful fight to regain the First Division status lost in 1977-78.

Bought from Charlton in May, 1967, for £50,000 no player could have given more valuable service to a club.

Full-back Frank Lampard, too, can never be accused of giving anything less than 100 per cent.

Before leaving his beloved Hammers after 16 years to take over as manager of England, Ron Greenwood said: "We have the most loyal supporters in the country. If anyone deserves success they do. And West Ham will give it to them — by playing football."

Under his successor John Lyall, The Hammers have done just that.

Alan Sealey (No. 8) beats the Munich 1860 goalkeeper Sealey scores his second goal in the European Cup Winners' Cup Final v. Munich 1960.

It has been my great pleasure, to say nothing of honour, over the last decade or so of football at the top level to play with some of the finest men in the game.

I have learned from and admired players with both Celtic and Scotland who have become legends. Whatever happens in my career now they can never take that away from me.

Of course there were others in my time who won my admiration, but because they were neither Celts nor Scots were never in the same eleven as my good self.

So I thought you might like a stroll down memory lane as I list my favourite team of players I have played with at some time, a line-up of Scots which I think could take on the best teams in the world.

'MY DREAM TEAM'

Of course I go for each of these players at their best although some are still playing and may still go on to greater things . . . and you will excuse me if I list myself at left-back. I couldn't bear to miss out playing in this side!

GOALKEEPER . . . It was tough and Ronnie Simpson, number one in Celtic's European Cup winning team nearly got my vote. But instead I will go for Alan Rough, Scotland's most capped 'keeper.

In spite of outrageous, unjustified criticism from people like TV man Bob Wilson who fail to see his weekly performances for Partick Thistle, Alan has proved that he is the best around. His razor sharp reactions and unflappable temperament are the big assets.

The rest of my team is in 4-3-3 formation.

RIGHT-BACK . . . My old friend and rival Sandy Jardine of Rangers. There is a little sentiment about this selection because I have partnered Sandy at international level more often than any other full-back. The big thing he has going for him is that remarkable attacking flair.

SWEEPER . . . Ice-cool Martin Buchan of Manchester United. His ability to read the game and his icy cool approach linked with an under-rated ability to tackle well win the vote ahead of such as big George Connelly.

CENTRE-HALF . . . Alan Hansen of Liverpool, but only just. This was the most difficult choice of all to make with candidates like Jim Holton, Gordon McQueen and the man who is now my boss, Billy McNeill. But Alan wins it

Tartan Talk
DANNY McGRAIN

because there is still so much potential there and there is no saying just how good he could get.

LEFT-BACK . . . Yours truly. It's my team, after all!

RIGHT MIDFIELD . . . A man whose career was ending just as mine began. The amazing Bobby Murdoch who used to hit these long fabulous passes with millimetre accuracy. There's not a manager who wouldn't give his eye teeth for a Murdoch now.

CENTRE MIDFIELD . . . Regular Tartan Talk readers will know that this is no contest. Davie Hay by a street. His determination and professionalism put him streets ahead of the rest. Oh, but for Davie in Argentina in 1978!

LEFT MIDFIELD . . . Former Scotland skipper Bruce Rioch wins it here. His shooting power and strength were first-rate, but Bruce's personality would be a big help to any team.

RIGHT WING . . . It took me all of half

a second to decide. Jimmy Johnstone whose ball control was so magical I swear he left stardust in his wake. Jinky is a living legend.

STRIKER . . . Again an easy choice. The King himself, Denis Law. He was my teenage idol and I could hardly believe it when I finally got to play in the same Scotland team. He could score goals others only dream about.

STRIKER . . . The finest player I have ever seen. Again it will come as no surprise to regular Tartan Talk customers that one Kenny Dalglish Esq. finds a place in my side. A match-winner.

SUBS . . . I would go for Joe Jordan and Bobby Lennox on the bench and that shows just what an incredible team I have put together if guys like that can't actually make a place.

Now, who's first for a game?

Kenny Dalglish . . . the greatest player McGrain has ever seen.

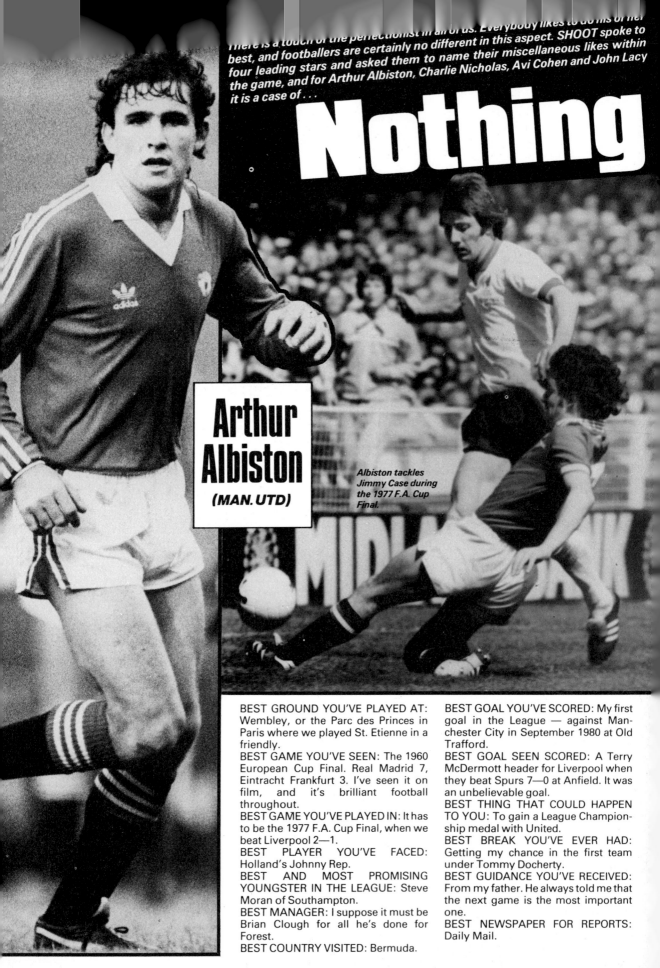

There is a touch of the perfectionist in all of us. Everybody likes to do his or her best, and footballers are certainly no different in this aspect. SHOOT spoke to four leading stars and asked them to name their miscellaneous likes within the game, and for Arthur Albiston, Charlie Nicholas, Avi Cohen and John Lacy it is a case of . . .

Nothing

Arthur Albiston
(MAN. UTD)

Albiston tackles Jimmy Case during the 1977 F.A. Cup Final.

BEST GROUND YOU'VE PLAYED AT: Wembley, or the Parc des Princes in Paris where we played St. Etienne in a friendly.

BEST GAME YOU'VE SEEN: The 1960 European Cup Final. Real Madrid 7, Eintracht Frankfurt 3. I've seen it on film, and it's brilliant football throughout.

BEST GAME YOU'VE PLAYED IN: It has to be the 1977 F.A. Cup Final, when we beat Liverpool 2—1.

BEST PLAYER YOU'VE FACED: Holland's Johnny Rep.

BEST AND MOST PROMISING YOUNGSTER IN THE LEAGUE: Steve Moran of Southampton.

BEST MANAGER: I suppose it must be Brian Clough for all he's done for Forest.

BEST COUNTRY VISITED: Bermuda.

BEST GOAL YOU'VE SCORED: My first goal in the League — against Manchester City in September 1980 at Old Trafford.

BEST GOAL SEEN SCORED: A Terry McDermott header for Liverpool when they beat Spurs 7—0 at Anfield. It was an unbelievable goal.

BEST THING THAT COULD HAPPEN TO YOU: To gain a League Championship medal with United.

BEST BREAK YOU'VE EVER HAD: Getting my chance in the first team under Tommy Docherty.

BEST GUIDANCE YOU'VE RECEIVED: From my father. He always told me that the next game is the most important one.

BEST NEWSPAPER FOR REPORTS: Daily Mail.

Avi Cohen ranks Holland's Rensenbrink highly.

Avi Cohen
(LIVERPOOL)

BEST GROUND YOU'VE EVER PLAYED ON: At Melbourne in Australia. It is a tremendous stadium.

BEST GAME YOU'VE SEEN: The 1979 F.A. Cup Final when Arsenal beat Manchester United 3—2.

BEST GAME YOU'VE PLAYED IN: For Liverpool in the 1—1 draw with Ipswich at Anfield in October 1980.

BEST PLAYER YOU'VE FACED: Holland's Robbie Rensenbrink.

BEST AND MOST PROMISING YOUNGSTER IN THE LEAGUE: Apart from our own Sammy Lee I would say Gary Shaw of Aston Villa.

BEST MANAGER: It would be impossible for me to say anyone other than Bob Paisley.

BEST COUNTRY VISITED: Australia.

BEST GOAL YOU'VE SCORED: For Maccabi Tel Aviv against Hapoel. We made a quick break and I hit a volley from 25 yards. We won that game 2—0.

BEST GOAL YOU'VE SEEN SCORED: The goals scored by Arie Haan for Holland against West Germany and Italy in the 1978 World Cup Finals.

BEST THING THAT COULD HAPPEN TO YOU: To win any honours with Liverpool.

BEST BREAK YOU'VE EVER HAD: Signing for Liverpool.

BEST GUIDANCE YOU'VE RECEIVED: A friend once told me never to give up, and to keep trying all the time even when I'm not in the team.

BEST NEWSPAPER FOR REPORTS: The Daily Mail.

Nothing but the best

Dundee United's Paul Hegarty usually gives Charlie Nicholas a few problems.

Charlie Nicholas
(CELTIC)

BEST GROUND YOU'VE PLAYED AT: Hampden Park. I'll be sorry when they finally pull it down.

BEST GAME YOU'VE SEEN: I have always been a Celtic supporter, and the best game I can remember was when they won the European Cup in 1967.

BEST GAME YOU'VE PLAYED IN: My debut for Celtic. We lost 2—1 in a European Cup tie away to Diosgyor of Hungary, but won the home leg to go through.

BEST PLAYER YOU'VE FACED: Dundee United's Paul Hegarty.

BEST AND MOST PROMISING YOUNGSTER IN THE LEAGUE: John MacDonald of Rangers and Alex McLeish of Aberdeen.

BEST MANAGER: I'll have to say Billy McNeill — I don't want to upset the boss!

BEST COUNTRY VISITED: Spain.

BEST GOAL YOU'VE SCORED: On my League debut v Partick. I bent a shot round Alan Rough.

BEST GOAL YOU'VE SEEN SCORED: Archie Gemmill's goal for Scotland in the 1978 World Cup against Holland. And one by Glenn Hoddle for Spurs against Manchester United.

BEST THING THAT COULD HAPPEN TO YOU: To win the European Cup with Celtic.

BEST BREAK YOU'VE EVER HAD: Getting into the Celtic side.

BEST GUIDANCE YOU'VE RECEIVED: Danny McGrain told me to keep my Scottish accent. As long as I don't try to change, I'll always keep my feet on the ground.

BEST NEWSPAPER FOR REPORTS: Daily Mirror.

BEST GROUND YOU'VE PLAYED AT: Wembley, when I played for Fulham in the 1975 F.A. Cup Final.

BEST GAME YOU'VE SEEN: The 1966 World Cup Final when England beat West Germany 4—2.

BEST GAME YOU'VE PLAYED IN: The F.A. Cup Semi-Final when we beat Birmingham in 1975.

BEST PLAYER YOU'VE FACED: Pele. I played against him when Santos met Fulham in a tour game.

BEST AND MOST PROMISING YOUNGSTER IN THE LEAGUE: Liverpool's Sammy Lee.

BEST MANAGER: Results speak for themself — it has to be Liverpool's Bob Paisley.

BEST COUNTRY VISITED: West Germany.

BEST GOAL YOU'VE SCORED: For Fulham against Southampton. It was one of the few I scored with my feet.

BEST GOAL SEEN SCORED: One by George Best which they occasionally show on TV. He picked the ball up on the half-way line, beat about five players and slid it into the corner of the net.

BEST THING THAT COULD HAPPEN TO YOU: For Spurs to win the double again.

BEST BREAK YOU'VE EVER HAD: Signing for Fulham at the comparatively late age of 20.

BEST GUIDANCE YOU'VE RECEIVED: Jim Clarkson, who used to run my college side and was also in charge of the London coaching clinics, helped me through all my problems.

BEST NEWSPAPER FOR REPORTS: The Sunday Times.

John Lacy
(SPURS)

great future at Anfield.

55

SOCCER SPECTACULAR

For the first time in over half a century of World Cup history, no fewer than 24 nations will be in Spain, aiming to carry off soccer's most glittering prize.

The bare statistics offer us an unprecedented bonanza of 52 matches in 29 days of competition, and the moguls of football's international governing body FIFA promise that these new super-enlarged World Cup Finals will treat us to a soccer spectacular such as we've never seen before. The Spaniards, who are organising the event, fervently agree — though perhaps with more hope than conviction.

On the other hand, many critics are already taking a more gloomy view, arguing that a quarter of the teams on show will be merely make-weights without the slightest hope of winning the trophy, and that our chances of witnessing an enthralling spectacle are therefore somewhat less than remote . . .

The tragedy is that the 1982 World Cup is the one that everybody wants to see. Countless thousands of fans from the 14 European nations who've qualified for the Finals have been dreaming of grabbing a unique chance to combine top football with the sun-soaked merriment of Spain's unrivalled holiday resorts. But the organisers have dashed the fans' dreams of sunshine, flamenco and football by simply accepting as a World Cup centre every city that asked to stage matches — even Malaga, where the La Rosaleda stadium was initially dismissed as totally inadequate by a FIFA inspection team.

As a result, supporters planning to travel to Spain find that the action has been fragmented into tiny bits and pieces in no fewer than 17 stadiums in 14 different cities. Only the six seeded teams avoid travelling during the first phase, and it's possible for a team reaching the Final to have played in five different cities and to have travelled around 2,000 miles in the process.

Not surprisingly, travel agents are having to ask four-figure prices if they're to offer packages covering all this flitting around inside Spain. And many fans are aghast at being asked to pay much the same prices to hop across the Channel as they paid to travel all the way to Argentina in 1978!

In fact, given the way the Finals have been organised, there seems little chance for fans to settle down anywhere — except in front of the television set! Mind you, even televiewers will be dismayed to see that, of the seven days with no football, three of the rest days fall at the weekend — exactly when most fans will be at home expecting to see some action!

The sad fact for World Cup aficionados is that only one of the 17 stadiums will stage more than three matches. And people who thought of installing themselves permanently in the major cities of Madrid or Barcelona will be disappointed to discover there's no football in either venue for two weeks.

To go into a little more detail, the 12 grounds to be used for the first phase have been split into six pairs. The Group 3 pair of Alicante and Elche are mercifully only 15 miles apart; and in Group 2 it's only a 19-mile hike from Gijon to Oviedo. But in Group 1, the grounds at Vigo and La Coruna are 76

(right) Argentina's Mario Kempes on the ball, chased by Holland's Willy Van der Kerkhof.

OR FOOTBALL FLOP?

ESPAÑA 82

miles apart; in Group 4 it's 175 miles from Bilbao to Valladolid or vice versa; 140 miles separate the Group 6 centres of Seville and Malaga; and Group 5 takes the biscuit, with no less than 205 miles separating Valencia and Zaragoza. Obviously these distances will not be a great inconvenience to the teams themselves — it's the poor fan who'll be hit by the costs of hopping from ground to ground!

Then, in the second phase, all the action shuts down abruptly in these centres and switches suddenly to Madrid and Barcelona. The Semi-Finals will be played simultaneously (and 650 miles part) in Barcelona and Seville; and the third and fourth place match will take place in one of the Mediterranean cities 24 hours before the Final in Madrid.

For the players themselves, the climate could present many more problems than the constant travelling. Take a look at the map and you'll see that most of the centres are dotted around the coastal fringes of Spain's

immense geography. But the Atlantic coast in the north is a vastly different proposition from the sunny Mediterranean cities. Up in the north, June temperatures are not a great deal higher than in Britain, and the weather is anybody's guess — except that two weeks without rain would be a turn-up for the book. Certainly British teams will feel more comfortable in these latitudes than in the 80-degree heat of the Mediterranean, though any team qualifying for the second phase must be prepared for an abrupt change of climate as the action moves south. Fortunately, the organisers have taken the climate into account when fixing kick-off times, with matches in the north starting at 5pm (4pm in Britain) and those in the "hot zone" kicking off at 9pm (8pm in Britain).

If the expansion of the Finals to 24 teams has created some unprecedented problems in the organisation of the tournament, the impact on the football itself remains something of an unknown quantity. Pessimists fear that the presence of six "minnows" from Asia, Africa and Central America instead of the traditional three will simply increase the number of meaningless matches involving teams who are unlikely to bring large numbers of supporters with them. We can only hope, for the tournament's sake, that some of these dark horses can follow Tunisia's example in 1978 and provide serious opposition to the more experienced Europeans and South Americans. With one "minnow" in each group, one can only hope that we have no repetitions of the ludicrous situation in 1974,

ZICO

when Yugoslavia, Brazil and Scotland drew with each other, and the group was decided purely on the number of goals each had put past poor Zaire.

And one can't help but fear that many matches will be played with one — or even both — teams intent more on avoiding defeat than on winning. Certainly in the first phase, where the top two teams qualify from each

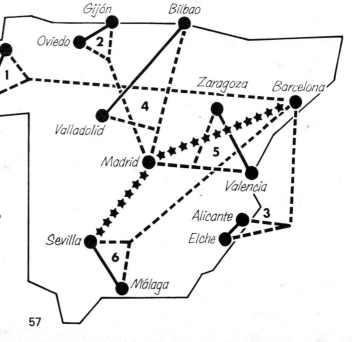

THIS MAP gives you some idea of the travelling fans and teams will have to do during the World Cup. The figures are the groups for the First Round of matches and centres for these games are linked by a solid line. For example, Group 1 is to be played in La Coruna and Vigo, Group Two in Oviedo and Gijon. The dotted lines indicate where the Group 1 winners will have to travel to play their Second Round matches. Group 1 go to Barcelona, Group 2 to Madrid, Group 3 from Alicante and Elche also to Barcelona and so on. The stars show where the Semi-Finals and Final will be played — Sevilla, Barcelona and Madrid.
(above) A model of the new stadium that will be built.

SOCCER SPECTACULAR OR FOOTBALL FLOP?

group, a lot of sides may well adopt safety-first tactics against the "quality" opposition and aim to run up a hefty goal difference against the minnows. Still, let's give the 24-team experiment a fair crack of the whip, and hope that the tournament is played in a more adventurous spirit than the 1980 European Championships . . .

Predictions are a dangerous occupation in football, but obviously World Champions Argentina will be keen to prove they can beat the best without the advantage of playing on their home soil. Menotti's young — but experienced — side will be the team everybody wants to beat, and we can only hope that their opponents don't react to the super skills of Diego

Maradona by trying to kick him off the park!

Host nation Spain will be expected to give good account of themselves, and manager Pepe Santamaria certainly has a lot of good youngsters at his disposal. Spain's traditional problem has been a lack of goal-power, thanks to the large number of imported strikers playing in Spanish teams, and they continue to produce their best results playing a defend-and-counter-attack game away from home. There's still a question mark over their ability to produce the goods at home when they're expected to make the running themselves, and one wonders whether the passionate support of the Spanish fans will help them lift their game or spoil their chances by putting the team under too much pressure.

Of the remainder, one can expect both West Germany and Brazil to be there or thereabouts — and let's hope that Brazilian ace Zico will finally unveil the full range of his talents on the international stage after a series of disappointing performances at the top level. The rest? Regrettably, they form a large pack of near-equal ability, and even the bookmakers are hard-pressed to draw many distinctions.

It's also interesting to speculate, if you're on form with your crystal ball, which new names will emerge as world superstars from the 1982 showpiece — just as Mario Kempes burst on the scene in 1978, and Bernd Schuster hit the headlines in a brief burst of super-play during the 1980 European Championship?

BERND SCHUSTER

The World Cup Schedule

FIRST PHASE

(24 teams split into six groups of four. Top two from each group qualify for next phase)

JUNE

Sunday	13	Opening match in Barcelona
Monday	14	One match in Group 1 (Vigo); Group 3 (Alicante); and Group 6 (Seville)
Tuesday	15	Games in Group 1 (Coruna); Group 3 (Elche); Group 6 (Malaga)
Wednesday	16	Group 2 (Gijon); Group 4 (Bilbao); Group 5 (Valencia)
Thursday	17	Group 2 (Oviedo); Group 4 (Valladolid); Group 5 (Zaragoza)
Friday	18	As for Mon. 14th
Saturday	19	As for Tues. 15th
Sunday	20	As for Weds. 16th
Monday	21	As for Thurs. 17th
Tuesday	22	As for Tues. 15th
Wednesday	23	As for Mon. 14th
Thursday	24	As for Thurs. 17th
Friday	25	As for Weds. 16th

SECOND PHASE

(12 teams split into four groups of three. Winner of each group qualifies for semi-finals)

Monday	28	One match in Group 1 (Barcelona), Group 4 (Madrid)
Tuesday	29	Group 2 (Madrid); Group 3 (Barcelona)

JULY

Thursday	1	Group 1 (Barcelona); Group 4 (Madrid)
Friday	2	Group 2 (Madrid); Group 3 (Barcelona)
Sunday	4	Group 1 (Barcelona); Group 4 (Madrid)
Monday	5	Group 2 (Madrid); Group 3 (Barcelona)
Thursday	8	SEMI-FINALS (Barcelona & Seville)
Saturday	10	3rd & 4th-place match (in the city where opening match would have taken place)
Sunday	11	FINAL (Madrid)

Previous Finalists

URUGUAY 1930

FINAL
URUGUAY 4, ARGENTINA 2 (1-2)

Uruguay: Ballesteros; Nasazzi (capt.), Mascheroni, Andrade, Fernandez, Gestido, Dorado, Scarone, Castro, Cea, Iriarte.

Argentina: Botasso; Della Torre, Paternoster, Evaristo J., Monti, Suarez, Peucelle, Varallo, Stabile, Ferreira (capt.), Evaristo M.

Scorers: Dorado, Cea, Iriarte, Castro for Uruguay; Peucelle, Stabile for Argentina.

Leading scorer: Stabile (Argentina) 8.

ITALY 1934

FINAL
ITALY 2, CZECHOSLOVAKIA 1 (0-0) (1-1) after extra time. *Rome.*

Italy: Combi (capt.); Monzeglio, Allemandi; Ferraris IV, Monti, Bertolini, Guaita, Meazza, Schiavio, Ferrari, Orsi.

Czechoslovakia: Planicka (capt.); Zenisck, Ctyroky, Kostalek, Cambal, Kreil; Junek, Svoboda, Sobotka, Nejedly, Puc.

Scorers: Orsi, Schiavio for Italy; Puc for Czechoslovakia.

Leading Scorers: Schiavio (Italy), Nejedly (Czechoslovakia), Conen (Germany) each 4.

FRANCE 1938

FINAL
ITALY 4, HUNGARY 2 (3-1). *Paris.*

Italy: Olivieri; Foni, Rava; Serantoni, Andreola, Locatelli; Biavati, Meazza (capt.), Piola, Ferrari, Colaussi.

Hungary: Szabo; Polgar, Biro, Szalay, Szuca, Lazar; Sas, Vincze, Sarosi (capt.), Szengelier, Titkos.

Scorers: Colaussi (2), Piola (2) for Italy; Titkos, Sarosifer for Hungary.

Leading Scorer: Leonidas (Brazil) 8.

BRAZIL 1950

FINAL POOL
Uruguay 2, Spain 2
Brazil 7, Sweden 1
Uruguay 3, Sweden 2
Brazil 6, Spain 1
Sweden 3, Spain 1
Uruguay 2, Brazil 1

FINAL POSITIONS

	P	W	D	L	F	A	Pts
Uruguay	3	2	1	0	7	5	5
Brazil	3	2	0	1	14	4	4
Sweden	3	1	0	2	6	11	2
Spain	3	0	1	2	4	11	1

Leading Scorers: Ademir (Brazil) 7, Schiatlino (Uruguay), Basora (Spain) 5.

SWITZERLAND 1954

FINAL
WEST GERMANY 3, HUNGARY 2

West Germany: Turek; Posipal, Kohlmeyer; Eckel, Liebrich, Mai; Rahn, Morlock, Walter, O., Walter, F. (capt.), Schaefer.

Hungary: Grosics; Buzansky, Lantos; Bozsik, Lorant, Zkarias; Czibor, Kocsis, Hidegkuti, Puskas (capt.), Toth, J.

Scorers: Morlock, Rahn (2) for Germany, Puskas, Czibor for Hungary.

Leading Scorer: Kocsis (Hungary) 11.

SWEDEN 1958

FINAL
BRAZIL 5, SWEDEN 2 (2-1) *Stockholm.*

Brazil: Gilmar; Santos, D., Santos, N.; Zito, Bellini, Orlando, Garrincha, Didi, Vava, Pele, Zagalo.

Sweden: Svensson; Bergmark, Axbom; Boerjesson, Gustavsson, Parliag, Hamrin, Gren, Simonsson, Liedholm, Skoglund.

Scorers: Vava (2), Pele (2), Zagalo for Brazil, Liedholm, Simonsson for Sweden.

Leading Scorer: Fontaine 13 (present record total).

CHILE 1962

FINAL
Santiago
BRAZIL 3, CZECHOSLOVAKIA 1 (1-1)

Brazil: Gilmar, Santos, D., Mauro, Zozimo, Santos, N.; Zito, Didi; Garrincha, Vavà, Amarildo, Zagalo.

Czechoslovakia: Schroiff; Tichy, Novak; Pluskal, Popluhar, Masopust, Pospichal, Scherer, Kvasniak, Kadraba, Jelinek.

Scorers: Amarildo, Zito, Vavà for Brazil, Masopust for Czechoslovakia.

Leading Scorers: Albert (Hungary), Ivanov (Russia), Sanches, L. (Chile), Garrincha, Vavà (Brazil), Jerkovic (Yugoslavia) each 4.

ENGLAND 1966

FINAL *Wembley*
ENGLAND 4, WEST GERMANY 2 (1-1) (2-2) after extra time.

England: Banks; Cohen, Wilson; Stiles, Charlton, J., Moore; Ball, Hurst, Hunt, Charlton, R., Peters.

West Germany: Tilkowski; Hottges, Schulz, Weber, Schnellinger; Haller, Beckenbauer; Overath, Seeler, Held, Emmerich.

Scorers: Hurst 3, Peters for England, Haller, Weber for Germany.

Leading scorer: Eusebio (Portgual) 9.

MEXICO 1970

FINAL *Mexico City.*
BRAZIL 4, ITALY 1.

Brazil: Felix, Carlos Alberto, Brito, Piazza, Everaldo; Gerson, Clodoaldo; Jairzinho, Pele, Tostao, Rivelino. No subs.

Italy: Albertosi; Burgenich, Cera, Rosato, Facchetti; Bertini, Riva; Domenghini, Mazzola, De Sisti, Boninsegna. Subs: Juliano for Bertini, Rivera for Boninsegna.

Scorers: Pele, Gerson, Jairzinho, Carlos Alberto for Brazil; Boninsegna for Italy.

Leading scorer: Muller (West Germany) 10.

WEST GERMANY 1974

FINAL
Munich
WEST GERMANY 2, HOLLAND 1 (2-1).

West Germany: Maier; Vogts, Schwarzenbeck, Beckenbauer, Breitner, Bonhof, Hoeness, Overath, Grabowski, Muller, Holzenbein.

Holland: Jongbloed; Suurbier, Rijsbergen (De Jong), Haan, Krol, Jansen, Van Hanegem, Neeskens, Rep, Cruyff, Rensenbrink (Van der Kerkhof R).

Scorers: Breitner *(pen),* Muller for West Germany, Neeskens *(pen)* for Holland.

Leading scorer: Lato (Poland) 7.

ARGENTINA 1978

FINAL
Buenos Aires
ARGENTINA 3, HOLLAND 1 (1-0) (1-1) after extra time.

Argentina: Fillol; Passarella, Olquin, Galvan (L), Tarantini, Ardiles (Larrosa), Gallego, Ortiz (Houseman), Bertoni, Luque, Kempes.

Holand: Jongbloed; Krol, Poortvliet, Brandts, Jansen (Suurbier), Haan, Neeskens, Van der Kerkhof (W), Rep (Nanninga), Van der Kerkhof (R), Rensenbrink.

Scorers: Kempes 2, Bertoni for Argentina; Nanninga for Holland.

Leading scorer: Kempes (Argentina) 6.

'FOR UNITED, SECOND

As a youngster I used to marvel at Manchester United. Just about every football fan had a soft spot for the club that not only survived the 1958 Munich Air Disaster — I was just coming into the world then! — but went on to become Champions of Europe.

When it became obvious that Chelsea and I would be parting company three or four clubs were interested in me . . . notably Ipswich, Everton and United.

Out of respect I listened to what the other clubs had to offer, but once United had come into the reckoning there was only one club for me. I would have been prepared to play another few months at Chelsea to join them. Thankfully, the clubs sorted out a fee and when I met Dave Sexton the rest was a formality.

Of course, I knew Dave from his Chelsea days. I was aware of his coaching ability, what he expected from players and how he liked his teams to perform. While simply playing for Manchester United F.C. was the biggest single influence in my signing, naturally the fact that Dave Sexton was manager was also a big help.

The first lesson any player coming to Old Trafford learns is that United are a big club. I thought I was aware of this, with the vast following and supporters clubs all over the world. Until you are actually a United player you simply

have no idea of the magnitude of the club.

The fans expect success — and success isn't finishing second in the League, qualifying for Europe or being runners-up in the F.A. Cup. Success is winning trophies. First is success and second is nowhere.

Chelsea are, in their own way, a big club with a traditional following. United are out on their own, though. Not only do the supporters demand success, they also want it achieved in style. The standards at Old Trafford are as high as you'll find anywhere.

This has its adverse effects, however. If we aren't one goal up inside ten minutes we can feel the pressure from the fans. Instead of playing our natural game, we tend to pump the ball upfield hopefully rather than build up our attacks with purpose.

Opponents invariably come to Old Trafford to defend, so life isn't always easy; I know the emphasis is on us to break down the opposing defence, but it can take longer than ten minutes.

LEFT . . . Wilkins waves to England fans during the disappointing European Championship.
BELOW . . . United's Red and White Army.

IS NOWHERE'

Ray Wilkins
WRITES FOR YOU

can't begin to explain the feeling of hopelessness and frustration under such circumstances.

I never want to go through a relegation again. While it's still mathematically possible to stay up there's hope, even though you know deep down the reality of the situation.

Once the nails are in your coffin it's

Playing in a side like United can only help me. Too often at Chelsea we had our backs to the wall and I was forced to adapt my game accordingly. Surrounded by so many good players at Old Trafford, I'm sure I can add new dimensions to my football.

I'd love to play in the World Cup Finals. I remember watching the '78 Finals and wishing how much England could have been there. It's the ultimate for any player.

I'm young enough to, hopefully, have another couple of opportunities after Spain '82. I recall Kevin Keegan saying to me how 1982 represents his last

Garry Birtles is outnumbered against Italy in Turin.

Fans everywhere are reluctant to give credit to the visiting team. If we don't win it's because we played badly — forgetting how well the other side may have played.

I'm not criticising our supporters. How could I with the backing they give us? Just illustrating what is expected of England's premier club.

I enjoyed my career at Chelsea. I couldn't have wished for a better soccer education. I grew up quickly in a soccer sense. Captain at 19, I experienced relegation and promotion . . . and finally relegation again, the season before I joined United.

The two lowest moments in my career were being relegated with Chelsea in 1979 and losing to Italy in the 1980 European Championship. Unless you've been through it, you

different. Motivation becomes much harder. You play for your pride as a professional, but knowing even if you win you can't really better yourself is an awful state of affairs.

I'm very aware of what is expected from a Manchester United player. I've had mixed luck since moving to Old Trafford. Things went well in my first season, when we almost pipped Liverpool for the title.

1980/81 was different though, and I missed half the season with a groin injury.

My ambition is to become the type of midfield player who dominates a game. It's been suggested that some of my passes are over-ambitious. Nothing gives me greater pleasure than to see Garry Birtles or Joe Jordan running on to one of my 40-yard throughballs. It was the same at Chelsea with Tommy Langley, who would run through a brick wall if needed.

chance to perform at the highest level.

The 1980 European Championship didn't go well for us. I still think back to our game against Belgium when Tony Woodcock had what everyone except the referee (yes, even the linesman) thought was a perfectly good goal disallowed. Who knows what we may have gone on to do?

Still, that's yesterday. Looking to the future I simply hope to win honours with Manchester United and England. Not original . . . but any medals will be very welcome!

PLAYING at Wembley, representing Scotland, performing in front of a frenzied tartan clad army of fans and emerging triumphant with an English scalp were all beyond the young coalminer's wildest, most romantic dreams.

He played football in the suffocating, hardly glamorous surroundings of trim Ochilview, home of Stenhousemuir. Within two years goalkeeper Stewart Kennedy was to catapult from this forgotten world of anonymity in the old Scottish Second Division, where fans are counted in hundreds rather than thousands, to play for his country against England.

His meteoric rise to fame was matched only by his rapid return to obscurity. The Scottish goalkeeper's jinx had claimed yet another victim!

Kennedy is a classic case of the hoodoo that seems to emerge whenever that Scottish goalkeeper's jersey is pulled over the head of some aspiring, and unsuspecting, youngster.

He was playing consistently well for Rangers — the club who paid Stenhousemuir a modest fee for the elastic-limbed number one to take him from Ochilview and the coal pits of Larbert to the big time setting of Ibrox — and there wasn't even the merest hint that the Wembley roof was about to cave in on him when he took the field with his colleagues in 1975.

Within minutes of the kick-off the three English goals swept past the luckless Kennedy as an uncontrollable tornado roared through the Scottish rearguard.

Since that sunny afternoon back in '75 Kennedy's career has hit a spiralling nosedive. He never really recovered. Although, to be fair, there were several other Scots on the field that afternoon who hardly performed to the peak of their capabilities.

Two years ago the big-time closed on Kennedy when he was given a free transfer and joined little Forfar. The roar of Wembley must seem like a million years away now as Kennedy plays in front of a handful of supporters at Station Park.

There are other goalkeepers who could tell the same tale of woe.

RIGHT ... Peter McCloy once handed Northern Ireland two goals.

'IS THERE A SCOTTISH

usually confident, competent Kennedy was stalking his goal-line as though he had been struck by a thunderbolt. He was a nervous, jittery, shambling figure staring a nightmare right in the face.

He stood utterly motionless as Gerry Francis fired England ahead with the first shot of the game in the opening minute. Hardly had he time to try to regather his nerves when Kevin Keegan curled over a lazy, looping cross from the right wing.

Kennedy started to come for the cross, changed his mind, hesitated and all was lost as rampaging Kevin Beattie outjumped Sandy Jardine and nodded the ball into the gaping net. Another

Aberdeen's Fred Martin had his reputation blown to smithereens when England thrashed seven goals past him at Wembley in another day of humiliation back in 1955.

Martin's blushes were saved slightly as one despairing Scottish fan said: "There's a newspaper strike on at the moment. Let's hope no one hears about this result!"

Frank Haffey left the same pitch resembling a dazed zombie when nine goals were walloped past him six years later.

He became the butt of many jokes of frustrated Scottish fans. All over Scotland Rangers fans blamed the

defeat on the Celtic goalkeeper.

The jokes were flying thick and fast. "Have you heard there's a new car on the market? It doesn't have a clutch. They're going to call it a Frank Haffey!"

"What time is it? Nine past Haffey ..."

The former Celt is now to be found living in Australia!

And so it went on as reputations were shot to smithereens while the individuals concerned were guarding their country's goal.

LEFT ... Fred Martin can only look on as one of England's seven goals go past him.
BELOW ... Peter Broadbent scores for England against Bill Brown in 1959.

Spurs' capable custodian Bill Brown took over from Haffey and, for a spell, the talk of hoodoos and jinxes came to a thankful end. But as Brown moved on the fans shuddered again at some horrible blunders that tragically marred some Scotland displays.

Adam Blacklaw of Burnley, and Liverpool's Tom Lawrence — two well-built, burly goalkeepers — were good and consistent team men, but they never really looked particularly safe whenever it came to taking over for their country.

A young Bobby Ferguson, who became Britain's most expensive goalkeeper at £65,000 when he moved from Kilmarnock to West Ham in 1967, came into the running, but he, too, fell victim of the 'keeper's curse.

Again England played a prominent part in his fall from international grace when he lost four goals at Hampden in '66. Scotland went down 4—3 in a

up-to-date, Kenny Dalglish, Steve Archibald, Andy Gray, Alan Hansen, Graeme Souness and Danny McGrain.

Ronnie Simpson, like Bill Brown before him, brought the sneers and the sniggers to an end, but, alas, Father Time eventually robbed him of his extraordinary talents and at the ripe old age of 39 he was forced to quit the game with a shoulder injury.

The X-certificate horror show for the Scottish fans was re-run as the frantic race for a suitable replacement for Simpson went on.

Jim Herriot, then playing for Birmingham City, was given the nod to see what he could do for his country, but in 1969 Wembley claimed another Scottish goalkeeper victim.

Herriot lost four goals in a 4—1 drubbing and never looked in the same class as the man at the other end, Gordon Banks. As Banks rose nonchalantly to pluck high balls out of the air with the ease and grace of an experienced campaigner, Herriot scampered

CONTINUED OVER

JINX ON KEEPERS?'

Saying a prayer? Ronnie Simpson in a thoughtful mood.

rollicking, rousing 90 minutes, but while the forwards seemed to be doing their job superbly well it appeared that every English effort was finding its way past Ferguson.

As one fan observed later: "If that game had lasted nine hours England would have won 99—98!"

Yet another epitaph was cruelly etched . . . yet another international career was wrecked.

The list seems endless; a long line of agony for Scots fans reflecting on what-might-have-been if only they had a 'keeper who could have matched the outfield class of players such as Denis Law, Jim Baxter, Pat Crerand, Jimmy Johnstone, Billy Bremner and, more along his line throwing hopeful punches at the ball praying that he might make contact. The comparison was not a good one. The end for Herriot was in sight...

Aberdeen's Bobby Clark came in and did exceedingly well, as did Hearts' Jim Cruickshank for a spell, but the old jinx raised its ugly head again in the early Seventies when Clark played in the Centenary match against England at Hampden.

In treacherous conditions, with a pitch more suited to alpine skiing, Clark lost five goals to England and his performance was sadly out of character.

"I try to forget all about that game," says the likeable Clark. "It was a terrible night all round and England adapted better to the pitch. They used the long ball all night and it had our defenders in constant trouble.

"Our lads tried to build up from the back, bringing the ball forward in stages, but it wasn't the night for text-book football.

"I'll never forget England's first goal that evening. I should have realised then that it was going to be a bad night. Peter Lorimer, a Scot with one of the hardest shots I have ever seen, took a swing at a cross by an English player and to my utter astonishment his 'clearance' rocketed over my head."

Rangers' Peter McCloy and Celtic's Ally Hunter started to put pressure on Clark for the number one position, but once they got their respective opportunities they must have wondered if it was all worthwhile!

RIGHT... Much criticised and underrated Alan Rough.
BELOW... Ally Hunter clears an England attack, but Scotland lost 1—0 in 1973.

McCloy had a nightmare evening against Northern Ireland in one of his first games. He practically gifted the Irish two goals and they stole away from Glasgow with both points.

Hunter came in, looked the part in his early matches, but was rather cruelly and harshly blamed for losing a goal in the vital World Cup-tie against Czecho-slovakia at Hampden in '73.

Nehoda, the tricky little Czech raider, sent in a wicked, dipping and swerving shot and Hunter looked agonisingly slow in diving for the ball. It crawled under his body and over the line and although Scotland went on to win 2—1 and book a place in the '74 Finals in West Germany Hunter was not even in the travelling squad.

David Harvey, Thomson Allan and Jim Stewart were the three 'keepers who went to West Germany and Harvey was reckoned to be the best in the tourney. He suffered as well, though, when Scotland slithered to a 2—1 European Championship defeat from Spain at Hampden on the team's return from the World Cup Finals and Partick Thistle's Alan Rough was soon given his chance to grab the problem spot.

The much-maligned Rough takes a philosophical view of his job for his country. He says: "I admit I have made mistakes, but which player hasn't?

"I've got more caps for my country than any other goalkeeper and that must testify to my ability."

Goalkeepers have formed a queue in their bid to take that place, haunted though it may be, from the Partick Thistle personality. George Wood knows all about the jinx after his flop against England at Wembley in '79 when he was blamed for at least two of England's three goals that afternoon.

Billy Thomson, once Rough's under-study at Thistle, also wants to add to his caps.

Scotland's last line of defence has so often been the laugh line of defence in the past. Alan Rough and Company have never seen that joke. They hope to have the last laugh...

When Graeme came in 'from the cold'

GRAEME Payne of Dundee United would have been forgiven for being slightly envious when Gordon Strachan picked up his well-merited Scottish Player of the Year award two seasons ago.

Payne, the Dundee United midfield mastermind, applauded as warmly as anyone as Aberdeen's Strachan was given the honour, but he must have thought of what might-have-been.

Strachan and Payne could be mistaken for twins. They are both the same size, possess the same build, have brilliant mops of bright red hair and are midfielders.

But when Strachan was gaining his plaudits, Payne was out in the cold wondering if there was any future for him with Dundee United.

Strachan was on his way to winning his first full Scottish international cap and had played a major role in Aberdeen's Premier League-winning title surge.

Payne had sat on the sidelines as Dundee United beat Aberdeen — Strachan and all! — 3—0 in the League Cup Final replay and there was to be no shock call into Jock Stein's international plans.

He had been on and off the transfer list without any great clamour for his signature. Payne might have been at his lowest ebb, but like the true battler he is, he fought his way back.

"I've been through hell with that player," says his manager Jim McLean. "It saddened me to leave him out of that League Cup-winning side because he is a player who has an array of talents . . . a player who has so much skill . . . a player who can entertain and excite."

Payne was in the middle of a form collapse at the time that Final was played, but, proving that lightning can strike twice in the same place, he was at his magnificent best a season later when United again won their way through to the Final of the League Cup to face Dundee at Dens Park.

"I was so delighted for Graeme that day," says Jim McLean. "When we first won the League Cup I wanted it for the players and the fans. When we won it the second time I wanted it for my family and Graeme Payne.

"He deserved that success. He plays football the way it should be played."

Payne shuns the bright lights off the pitch and says: "I'll always treasure the memory of that day when we beat Dundee 3—0 — when I came in from the cold. It was great to take part in such an historic occasion for the club.

"Now I've tasted that sort of success I want more . . . a lot more."

It could be that Gordon Strachan and Graeme Payne might well get together to fuse their colossal talents in the international side. That can only be good news for Scottish soccer fans . . . and disastrous news for rival defences.

Graeme Payne (third from right) celebrates helping Dundee United beat their neighbours of Dundee in the League Cup Final.

**DAVID
HODGSON
Middlesbrough**

Two of the League's most experienced campaigners — Stoke City defender Mike Doyle (stripes) and Norwich striker Joe Royle.

In the late forties and early fifties the total of spectators at League games was over 40 million a season. But as the years have passed so have the crowds dwindled. At the end of the 1979-80 season the grand total was only 24 and a half million.

What has happened during the past thirty years? Where have the fans gone? There are various reasons. Some blame the extensive TV coverage of top matches, others that ground prices have risen too high, but isn't the real reason the fact that the game itself is not such a crowd-pleasing spectacle? Football crowds have always loved goals and goalscorers — the more goals the better. But in the modern game goals have become a commodity in short supply, and all because of the modern idea among managers and players that defence is more important than attack.

In days gone by teams lined up with two full-backs, three half-backs and five forwards. Nowadays too often away teams concentrate on three men at the back covering their 'keeper, a midfield wall of five, leaving two in attack. Is it any wonder that there are quite a number of matches in which the two goalkeepers hardly have enough work beneath the bar to keep themselves warm.

Let's take a look at a few of the great differences between modern goals totals and those the jubilant, excited fans watched in the past. In 1961 when Spurs won the Championship they scored 115 goals in their 42 games. The grand total of goals in Division One that season was 1,724. That season Bobby Smith, England centre-forward,

scored 28 goals, Les Allen (father of Clive) 23, Welshman Cliff Jones 15, John White 13 and little Terry Dyson 12 — 91 goals from those five forwards. Note that two of them, Cliff Jones and Terry Dyson, were the wingers, and that proves one of the falacies of the modern game. Few teams now include two ORTHODOX wingers so strikers must now battle alone or snap up chances provided from their middlemen.

By the way, Spurs also won the Cup that season to complete a glorious ''double' and on their way to the Final they scored 19 goals. Compare those goal figures with the 1979-80 season when Spurs scored a mere 52 in the League. Incidentally, on the way to their 1961 Championship Spurs failed to score in only two of their 42 League

games. In the 1979-80 campaign the figure was twelve!

Here's another reason why goals totals are now lower than ever before. In the 1951-52 season there were 80 no-score draws. The 1979-80 campaign produced 184 games without a solitary goal!

When was the last time that a side scored a century of goals in a season? Not for a long, long time, although Lincoln City did it in 1976, but that was in Division Four when they romped away with the Championship of a very poor lowest Division season. But between 1925 and the early Sixties hardly a season passed without at least one centurion side. Sixty goal-hundreds were recorded during that period. Going even farther back we find that in

TON-UP TEAMS
Those who scored a soccer century in a season...

the 1930-31 season EIGHT clubs topped the hundred goals — Arsenal, Aston Villa and Sheffield Wednesday in Division 1; Everton (Division 2); Crystal Palace (Division South), and Chesterfield, Lincoln City and Tranmere (Division 3 North) . . . 898 goals in all. No wonder attendance figures broke all records that season.

But just one season later another EIGHT centuries were achieved — Everton, Aston Villa, Wolves, Fulham, Coventry, Plymouth, Lincoln and Tranmere. Staggering, isn't it?

In the 1956-57 season all four Division Champions topped the 100 goals target — Manchester United (Div.1); Leicester City (Div.2); Ipswich (Div.3 South) and Derby County (Div.3 North). The following season also had its dramatic

The Gunners last took the Championship title in 1970-71 they did it with a mere 71 goals, Ray Kennedy top scoring with 19.

The fading out of the orthodox centre-forward, the player whose sole purpose was to snap up the final pass from colleagues and bang the ball into the net, has had much to do with the lack of goals in recent years. What a fillip would be given to the modern game if men like Arthur Rowley, Brian Clough, Ted MacDougall and, going even further back, Nat Lofthouse and Stan Mortensen, to name but a few, could be rejuvenated! Those men, goal-hunters, were idols and wherever they played the fans turned up in their thousands.

It is quite obvious that if modern-

playing methods continue we shall not see beaten the record of the late Dixie Dean of 60 League goals for Everton in the 1927-28 season, a fantastic record following the equally incredible the previous season of 59 goals by George Camsell of Middlesbrough. Just compare those figures with the 1979-80 season when the League's leading scorer was Clive Allen, of Queens Park Rangers, with 28 goals. The nearest anyone has come to approaching those prolific performances was Terry Bly's 52 goals for Peterborough in 1960-61. The last man to score 40 goals in a League season was Ted MacDougall, of Bournemouth, with 42 goals.

Brian Clough must have nostalgic memories of the days when he was one of the most dynamic goalgetters in

Left: Spurs' Bobby Smith scores the first goal in his club's 1961 F.A. Cup Final win over Leicester City. Above: Lincoln City's Dick Kryzwicki hits one of the Fourth Division outfit's century of goals in their 1976 Championship season. Right: The late Dixie Dean, scorer of a record 60 goals in a season.

hundreds. Wolves were League Champions with 103 goals, followed by Preston North End with 100. West Ham were top of Division Two with 101 goals and Charlton finished third with 107. Yet the previous season they had finished bottom of Division 1 with 120 goals put past their 'keepers! Here's another staggering fact from the 1957-58 campaign. Manchester City scored 104 goals but had exactly 100 banged into their net.

So they had almost as many jeers as cheers!

When Arsenal were the greatest team in Britain during the 1930's, Champions four times in five seasons, they scored a grand total of 435 goals, including three centuries in the ''goals for'' column. They were the glory days of such men as David Jack, the mighty Ted Drake, Cliff Bastin and mercurial Joe Hulme, dynamic goalgetters. When

the game. During seven seasons between 1957 and 1963 Brian hit 193 League goals for Middlesbrough and 53 for Sunderland, a total of 246 before the tragic injury that brought his incredible career to an end.

Around that same period another of the game's greatest goal-kings was Arthur Rowley. During his memorable career with West Brom, Leicester and Shrewsbury he collected 434 League goals, a figure that may never be beaten.

In the 1960-61 season 63 players each collected more than 20 goals and in the next campaign twenty players scored 628 goals between them, their individual totals being between 24 and 41. Yet during the 1979-80 season only eight men scored 20 goals for their clubs.

So the message to today's managers and coaches is clear: abandon ''safety first'' soccer with its emphasis on defence and switch to an all-out attacking policy of 2-3-5 which will bring back the goals — and the missing fans!

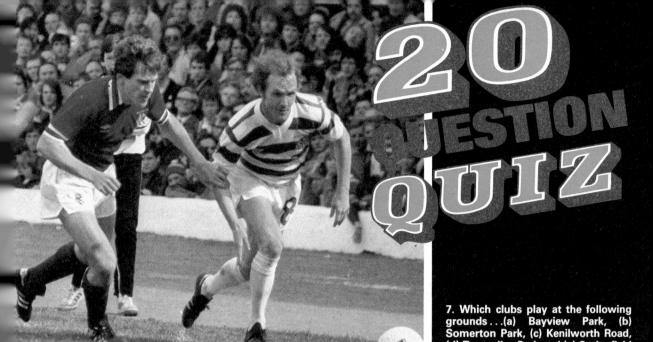

20 QUESTION QUIZ

7. Which clubs play at the following grounds . . .(a) Bayview Park, (b) Somerton Park, (c) Kenilworth Road, (d) Tannadice Park and (e) Springfield Park?

8. Cyrille Regis (below) was spotted by West Bromwich Albion playing for Southern or Isthmian League side Hillingdon Borough or Hayes?

1. Rangers and Celtic (above) clashed in the 1980 Scottish Cup Final at Ibrox. The game was decided in extra-time when Celtic scored through which player?

2. Still in Scotland, Dundee United retained the League Cup in 1980 when they beat neighbours Dundee 1—0, 2—0 or 3—0 at Dens Park?

3. The following players were transferred during 1980—81. Their former clubs are in brackets . . .can you name the ones they joined? (a) Terry Fenwick (Crystal Palace), (b) Gerry Armstrong (Tottenham) and (c) Tommy Hutchison (Coventry City).

4. Nottingham Forest failed to win their third consecutive Football League Cup when they lost 1—0 to Wolves in the 1980 Final at Wembley. Did Andy Gray score the only goal in the first or second-half?

5. Who took over the temporary managership of Crystal Palace when Terry Venables left to join Queens Park Rangers?

6. West Germany beat Belgium 2—1 in the Final of the 1980 European Championship. Which German player (below, number nine) scored both their goals?

15. Did Trevor Brooking score the winning goal for West Ham (above, with the trophy) against Arsenal in the 1980 Wembley F.A. Cup Final with a right foot shot or a header?

16. Manchester City's Ray Ranson (below) made his League debut at home to Nottingham Forest, Leicester City or Norwich City in December, 1978?

17. If the 1970 Football League Champions entertained the 1980 Scottish Premier Division Champions in a friendly which two clubs would be in opposition?

18. Peter McCloy was a regular member of which Scottish Premier Division club during the 1980—81 season?

19. True or false? The red and yellow cards, used by Football League referees, were discarded in January, 1980.

20. The 1980-81 League Cup competition produced plenty of shocks and surprises. (a) The outstanding result was Watford's 7—1 home victory against which First Division club, (b) can you name the two losing Semi-Finalists, (c) the Final, between Liverpool and West Ham, ended 1—1 at Wembley. Did David Johnson play for Liverpool in that game, and (d) Ipswich Town were knocked out in the Fourth Round by Birmingham City 2—1 at St. Andrews. Did Frank Worthington or Alan Ainscow score the winning goal in the second-half?

9. Brian Kidd (above) played for four other League clubs before joining Bolton. Can you name them?

10. Uruguay beat Brazil 1—0, 2—1 or 3—2 to win the Final of the Gold Cup, a competition between past World Cup winners, excluding England, in Montevideo in January, 1981?

11. Davie Sneddon was sacked as manager of which Scottish Premier Division club last season?

12. The following players were sent-off during the 1980—81 season . . .can you name the clubs for whom they were playing? (a) Eric Gates, (b) Terry Curran, (c) Paul Richardson, (d) Martin O'Neill and (e) Frank Worthington?

13. Who did Bob Paisley replace as manager of Liverpool in 1974?

14. This midfield star began his career with Morton before going South to join Spurs. From the North London club he went to Bolton and then Brighton. Can you identify him?

Arsenal's number eight, Alan Sunderland, heads past Ipswich 'keeper Paul Cooper to notch up the goal that enabled his club to gain a 1—1 draw at Highbury in the League last season.

TALES BEHIND

Manchester City's Phil Boyer finds a gap in the Spurs defence to head a spectacular goal. Unfortunately for him, it was City's only goal, and Spurs succeeded in scoring twice.

Alan Lee of Chelsea is at the far post to nod home one of the goals against Grimsby Town at Stamford Bridge. The London Blues won 3—0.

THE HEADERS...

Aberdeen have set Scotland alight in recent seasons, and one of their key players is Drew Jarvie, seen here scoring against Rangers with a textbook header demonstrating position, power and control.

Justin Fashanu on the ball for England Under-21's against Rumania.

Arsenal captain David
O'Leary close-marks Spurs'
Garth Crooks.

I 'll be 28 when my present Wolves contract expires. At that age I'll still be young enough to negotiate a new contract, be it with Wolves or another club. I can't really think that far ahead.

Despite some untimely injuries, I consider myself lucky because football has given me far more ups than downs ... more happiness than disappointments.

There isn't much I'd change if I had the chance to start my career all over again. I would certainly not have retaliated when Ondrus of Czechoslovakia clouted me in a 1978 World Cup qualifying tie, which resulted in a sending-off (the ref had no alternative) and a three-match ban.

'Why I said no to West Germany'

Andy Gray WRITES FOR YOU

And again I would refuse the offer from West German club Schalke 04. It was in 1975 and I was still a Dundee United player when the club came in for me.

Their terms were very attractive. Staggering in fact. Officials of the club treated me like a king — I couldn't have asked for better treatment.

However, I decided that as a teenager I wasn't ready for such a big step. Remember, it wasn't 'fashionable' for British players to move abroad then and I felt the next step in my career should be the English Football League, not the West German Bundesliga.

I wasn't aware of it at the time, but Aston Villa manager Ron Saunders was also tracking me. I remember United manager Jim McLean calling me to his office on the Friday. When a player receives such an order the news is invariably bad.

I thought I was going to be dropped!

Instead, he just asked me where he could get in touch with me later if he wanted to. I then thought that if I was going to be dropped he might at least have the courage to tell me to my face, not over the phone!

I couldn't have been more wrong! Well — almost. I wasn't playing against Celtic because I had to rush to the Midlands to meet Ron Saunders.

In my excitement, I didn't even have time to phone home to tell my mother my decision and she heard it on TV that I'd signed.

I enjoyed my spell with Villa. The team that won the League Cup in 1977 was,

potentially, the best seen in England during the 70's. Sadly, for one reason or another, it didn't stay together long enough to achieve this.

Even so, I established myself as one of England's top strikers and the double award of Young Player and Players' Player of the Year is still my most cherished football moment. Recognition by your fellow professionals in such a way must be the ultimate.

The following season didn't go well for me. I had more knocks and injuries then than in all my career put together.

Even so, when Ally MacLeod came round to announcing his Scotland squad for the

1978 World Cup in Argentina I was fit and looking forward to being selected.

He didn't think I was fully fit and I was left out. People said to me afterwards that I was better off out of it ... that there would be other opportunities.

How can anyone guarantee World Cup qualification? I would have loved to have been in Argentina, regardless of what happened over there. I may never have a similar opportunity, although I naturally hope one comes my way.

I should have more Scotland caps than I do and I feel I still have some lost time to make up for in this respect.

Still, when I look back over my career I've not done badly. I've played on the winning side in a Wembley Cup Final, scoring the only goal, too.

It's a great feeling and it's one I hope to repeat before I finally hang up my boots.

Andy Gray

MICK ROBERTSON
Brighton

Northern Ireland captain Martin O'Neill in the thick of the action against Sweden in a World Cup qualifier.

Triumph and tragedy for Allen

ALAN SNEDDON of Hibs is one player who will surely testify to soccer being a topsy-turvy profession where anything can, and often does, happen with unexpected and unwanted abruptness.

Only seven months after establishing himself as Celtic's regular right-back and playing superbly in the 1—0 Scottish Cup Final victory over Rangers in the riot-torn Hampden collision, Sneddon was collecting his boots and leaving Parkhead for the last time!

A swift £60,000 transfer took him to Hibs and Sneddon says: "Obviously I didn't figure in Bily McNeill's plans at Celtic and a move was the best idea for myself and the club.

"I enjoyed myself with Celtic — they are a marvellous club with superb fans — but now I am dedicated to the cause of Hibs. They pay my wages now and manager Bertie Auld is ambitious for the club to climb back to the top.

"I'm sure they will make it. That's why I was so happy to join such a progressive, go-ahead set-up. Easter Road is a place where things will happen in the future and I just aim to be there when they do."

Sneddon might have been surprised at the decline in his fortunes at Parkhead, but the entertaining right-back couldn't have been too shocked. After all, he had already tasted disappointment in his soccer career before going to Parkhead.

Alan, in fact, trained with Celtic's bitter enemy Rangers as an amateur, but never got the call-up at Ibrox. He went to Junior soccer, made a name for himself with Larkhall Thistle and did enough to persuade Celtic's former manager Jock Stein that he had what it takes to make a hit in the top grade.

'Great Night'

Stein signed the stylish Sneddon and within a season he was in the first team. His rocket-like rise to fame might have left him breathless, but he was determined not to be an overnight sensation.

"I'm always looking for consistency," he says. "The most important game is the next one. You can never rest on your laurels in football. Every new game is a different challenge, another hurdle to take."

Two seasons ago Sneddon was the toast of the Celtic fans when he outplayed Real Madrid's English international winger Laurie Cunningham in the European Cup Quarter-Final tie at Parkhead.

"That was a great night," he recalls. "We won 2—0 and I had a hand in both our goals. The first came when I fired in a low cross and the goalkeeper couldn't hold it. George McCluskey tucked it away from close range.

"The second came after I sent in a long cross. Johnny Doyle outjumped two of their defenders to send a header raging into the net. Alas, we came back to earth with a bump when we lost 3—0 in the second-leg. That still remains one of my biggest disappointments in the game. A tragedy that overshadowed our triumph."

Alan Sneddon, a colourful, cavalier of a full-back, has had more than his share of disappointments. It's time football smiled on this entertaining young man . . .

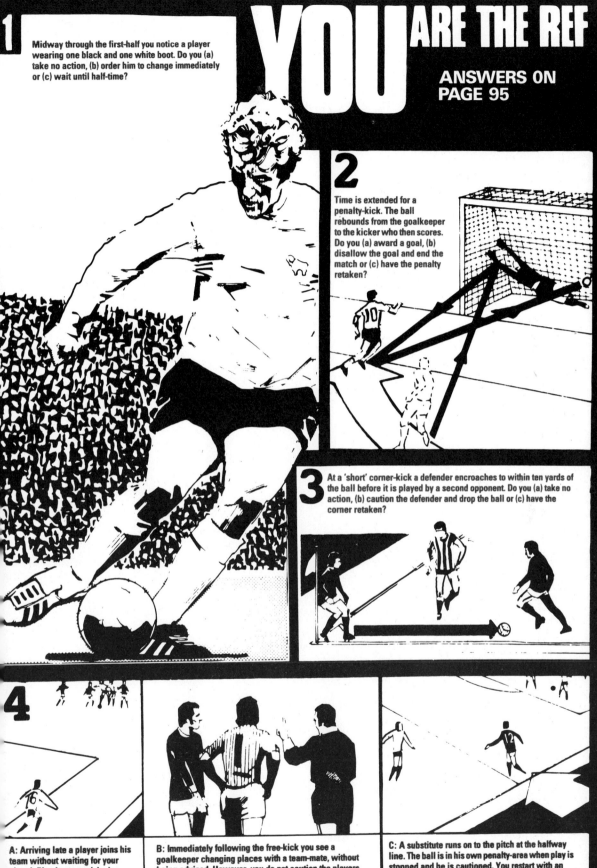

YOU ARE THE REF

1 Midway through the first-half you notice a player wearing one black and one white boot. Do you (a) take no action, (b) order him to change immediately or (c) wait until half-time?

ANSWERS ON PAGE 95

2 Time is extended for a penalty-kick. The ball rebounds from the goalkeeper to the kicker who then scores. Do you (a) award a goal, (b) disallow the goal and end the match or (c) have the penalty retaken?

3 At a 'short' corner-kick a defender encroaches to within ten yards of the ball before it is played by a second opponent. Do you (a) take no action, (b) caution the defender and drop the ball or (c) have the corner retaken?

4

A: Arriving late a player joins his team without waiting for your signal. Play is stopped, he is cautioned, and an indirect free-kick awarded where he was when the game was halted.

B: Immediately following the free-kick you see a goalkeeper changing places with a team-mate, without being advised. However, you do not caution the players until the ball goes out of play.

C: A substitute runs on to the pitch at the halfway line. The ball is in his own penalty-area when play is stopped and he is cautioned. You restart with an indirect free-kick where he was when play was stopped.
(Which of these procedures is incorrect?)

He can expect stiff competition from a talented gallery of managers all with qualifications worthy of the closest consideration from the F.A. officials who will go into a huddle at Lancaster Gate.

Let us consider the candidates, some of whom might seem surprise choices at first glance, yet have that thoroughbred pedigree essential to a demanding, often lonely, but rewarding job.

Clear favourite is BOBBY ROBSON, the man who guided Ipswich Town from the backwaters of East Anglia to European competition through the most colourful chapter in the First Division club's history.

of managers who have had less than five years experience in charge of clubs.

Lawrie McMenemy, like Robson, was a candidate to succeed Don Revie when he walked out on England.

He failed that time but could well get the nod next time he pushes his tall frame into Lancaster Gate for an interview.

His pedigree in management is impressive after building Southampton into the most successful side on the south coast on limited resources.

His capture of the breathtaking talents of Kevin Keegan was the coup of 1980, and if England are to recapture their capacity for scoring goals, perhaps

WHO NEXT FOR BOBBY ROBSON

"We don't want Ron Greenwood's job. He should carry on in control of the national team long after 1982 and even 1986 if necessary . . ."

The words of Bobby Robson, Manager of the England B team, and favourite to take charge of England if Ron Greenwood decides to retire from the job he has performed since 1977.

The only certainty about the most important job in English football is that the F.A., will have to put their heads together sometime in the next few years to find a successor to the former West Ham manager.

Their task will not be easy, for even the best League club manager in the land might not necessarily have the right qualities to run the national side.

So, who are the candidates for a job that has been occupied by only a select few since the War? Walter Winterbottom had the distinction of becoming England's first full-time manager before handing over to Alf Ramsey, later to be knighted for masterminding England's World Cup success in 1966.

Ramsey's departure heralded the arrival of Don Revie, the highly successful Leeds United manager. Revie's reign was brief and laced with controversy until his shock resignation in the summer of 1977.

Genial Joe Mercer did a caretaker's job until the F.A. decided to offer the job to Ron Greenwood.

Finding a successor to Greenwood will be equally onerous and when Bobby Robson, the England B team manager, said that the current England manager should not retire in haste he echoed the view of many people in the game.

"Ron's done a good job, whatever people say, in difficult circumstances," says Robson, making light of the fact that he himself is considered favourite to take over.

The men in charge of England's Under-21 side . . . Terry Venables and Dave Sexton.

His special talent is that he built a team on a small bank balance, relying on shrewd transfer dealings and a priceless talent for coaching.

Greenwood's philosophy for producing teams playing good football is Robson's and like the England manager he does not allow theory to stifle natural talent.

Robson has the "ear" of the players. He talks their language and they respect the former West Brom and Fulham player's judgement. He made 20 appearances for England as a wing-half and is familiar with the lifestyle at international level.

Robson remains totally convinced that whoever gets the job should have had lengthy experience of management. "We don't want someone who is still wet behind the ears, do we?" he says in response to suggestions that it might go to England's younger breed

the genial McMenemy is the answer.

Goal-power is a feature of all McMenemy teams. They might concede a few in their quest for attack but Southampton's players have been taught the way to goal by the former Guardsman from Geordie-land.

Brian Clough has confessed that he is less interested in the England job than he was at the time of Revie's resignation. His credentials for leading England back to the top in world football would appear to be well established. Clough is another manager who has turned a quiet backwater into a hotbed of soccer.

Nottingham Forest were an ordinary side with few ambitions when Cloughie took charge after managerial service at Derby County, Brighton and Leeds United.

His skill in turning a struggling League club into European champions is a fairytale in itself. His motivation of players is unquestioned. Given the best players in the land, success is unlikely to elude him. The only question mark against Clough is in his attitude towards officialdom.

Directors knock before entering his office at the County Ground. Whether F.A. officials would take kindly to his rather dictatorial manner when he is running a football team is a challenge we might have an opportunity to witness.

One major point in his favour — he has rarely run a bad side even when cash has been in short supply.

John Bond's blood transfusion for an ailing Manchester City in the 1980-81 season will place him firmly in the minds of those sitting in judgement on the England job.

He is a winner, his teams attack positively, and there will be no lack of flair if John Bond is given the job.

Bond is another general from the old

West Ham academy of managerial talent. Malcolm Allison, Ron Greenwood, John Lyall and Phil Woosnam have all taken top jobs in football since their playing days at Upton Park.

When Ron Greenwood was criticised for England's poor performance in the 1980 European Championships in Italy, some of his detractors suggested a younger man should take control of the national side.

Terry Venables was their champion. Young, fresh faced, full of bright ideas and a bundle of energy at the helm at Crystal Palace. Ever mindful of the need for young talent, Ron Greenwood had recruited Venables' services for his England Under-21 sides.

Now, some said, was the time for "Venners" to be given his head. After all, they argued, he was more likely to have an affinity with the England players than a man almost twice his age.

The campaign, sounded out in the newspapers, gained little support and lost momentum totally when Venables left Palace to take charge of Queens Park Rangers in an overnight move which mystified many of his supporters.

There is no doubting Venables' qualities, and if he has the patience, his turn will no doubt come. If not next time then possibly the time after.

According to Bobby Robson, the job is not for a "young man" with only a year or two of experience of club management.

Howard Kendall and Geoff Hurst have shown enormous potential in raising the hopes of Blackburn Rovers and Chelsea respectively. They show the depth of talent the F.A. will have at their disposal in the years ahead.

They are no more than lukewarm contenders for the job. Ron Atkinson, boss at West Bromwich Albion and one of the best football brains in the country is a wholehearted disciple of the Greenwood regime and is often to be seen at the England hotel when they travel abroad.

He will talk football till midnight and long after if given the chance and will no doubt pitch for the job should cir-

THE ENGLAND JOB?
THE FAVOURITE

cumstances be right when it becomes available.

Not such a long-shot for the job is Dave Sexton, Manchester United's kindly manager with a depth of knowledge about the game that astounds his contemporaries.

He has tackled his job as manager of the England Under-21 side with enthusiasm and no lack of talent. He is one of Europe's best coaches, and if he lacks some of Brian Clough's ebullience, he compensates for it by getting close to his players.

If players speak highly of a manager he is half-way to succeeding in one of the most onerous jobs in the world.

But perhaps the man with the best pedigree, the best track record, a man of proven integrity, and the best qualified to succeed Ron Greenwood will NOT be in the running when the chair becomes vacant.

Bob Paisley, manager of Liverpool, is unlikely to want the job. He has all the credentials but to take him out of his beloved Anfield after 30 years would be as unthinkable as moving Nelson's Column to Salisbury Plain.

Could he persuade England to scale the heights his players have achieved at club level? It is a question to spark deep and speculative comment in any pub bar but one which is unlikely to be answered.

England might not have blazed a particularly handsome trail since winning the World Cup in 1966, but there is no shortage of talent available to the Football Association in their search for glory at international level in the last 20 years of this century.

Cometh the hour, cometh the man, probaby from the talented pack above.

Bobby Robson makes a point to Eric Gates during an Ipswich training session.

YULE

'Isn't Big Joe carrying the Christmas spirit a bit too far?'

'Boss, you told me to get some little crackers for the team's Christmas get-together . . .'

'The name's Father Christmas'

LAUGH...

'Is the new managing director handing out any rises?'

'Play like that again, and I'll put *you* on top of the Christmas tree'

'Perhaps if we put holly in their tracksuits they'd train harder'

'Just what I wanted, dear. A gold-plated pencil sharpener'

PROMOTION AND RELEGATION RECORDS

TENTH OF A GOAL SAVED NEWCASTLE

In recent years many of the big clubs, traditionally members of the First and Second Divisions, have for the first time experienced football in the lower reaches of the League. Famous names like Preston North End, Aston Villa, Blackburn Rovers, Bolton Wanderers, Huddersfield Town and Sheffield Wednesday.

Another of the most successful clubs — four times League Champions, twice runners-up; six times F.A. Cup winners and five times Finalists, had the narrowest of escapes from a drop into the Third Division in 1937-38. That club is Newcastle United.

When the Geordies had completed their most disastrous season with a 4—1 defeat at Luton in May, 1938, it needed some calculations to decide who was going to take the drop along with Stockport County who had only 31 points. Just above them were three clubs with 36 points — Newcastle United, Nottingham Forest and Barnsley. Newcastle beat the other two by less than a tenth of a goal and Barnsley went down with Stockport.

TWO FROM 13

The keenest relegation struggle ever seen in the Football League was that in the First Division in 1927-28. With each club having only a couple of games to play any two of 13 could be relegated! When the games were completed there were no less than seven clubs on 39 points, one with 38 and one with 37. Among those threatened Manchester United finished strongest with three wins in a row, but Spurs and Middlesbrough each lost their last two games and were relegated.

VITAL PENALTY MISS

You have heard the saying "falling between two stools," well that is exactly what happened to Manchester City at the end of season 1925-26. They were narrowly beaten by Bolton Wanderers in the F.A. Cup Final, David Jack getting the only goal 12 minutes from time, and a week later were relegated from the First Division because they missed a penalty.

City only needed to draw that final game at Newcastle to avoid the drop into the Second Division, but they were beaten 3—2 and it was an especially unhappy occasion for Sid Austin who missed that penalty by shooting straight at the goalkeeper.

Everyone sympathised with the City's outside-right in having to take a penalty at such a critical point in the club's history, and although a goal would have saved the club from relegation it had to be admitted that City scarcely deserved a point from this game in which Newcastle's centre-forward, the inimitable Hughie Gallacher, (below) scored a brilliant hat-trick.

'HAT TRICK' FOR ERNIE

Footballers obviously derive great satisfaction from helping their club win promotion, but what about the player who helped three clubs win promotion IN THE SAME SEASON! Sounds impossible, but winger Ernie Shepherd achieved this distinction in 1948-49.

Ernie had been with Fulham since before the War, but after playing seven Second Division games for them at the start of 1948-49 he was transferred during December to West Bromwich Abion. There he made another four Second Division appearances before moving on to Hull City in March and completing the season with a half-dozen appearances for them in Division III(N). He actually scored with his first kick for the Boothferry Park club.

That season Fulham and West Bromwich Albion were promoted to the First Division and Hull City moved up into Division Two.

OWLS — COMEBACK CHAMPS

Sheffield Wednesday are champs among clubs that have regained First Division status only 12 months after relegation, for they have performed this feat four times. The

Owls did it in 1899-1900 following a big shake-up of the club and a move to their present ground. They did it again in 1951-52, thanks largely to the remarkable transformation wrought by Derek Dooley (above) who scored 46 Second Division goals in the promotion campaign. Down again three seasons later they bobbed up once more in 12 months with Roy Shiner and Albert Quixall getting most of their goals. Only two seasons later the pendulum swung back and they were relegated. Yet the following season that pendulum kept on swinging and Roy Shiner shot them back into the First Division with the able assistance of such stars as Peter Swan, Ron Springett, Redfern Froggatt and John Fenton.

CLOSE RACE

One of the tightest promotion races at the top of the Second Division was that in season 1909-10. On the last day four clubs were in with a chance — Manchester City, Oldham Athletic, Hull City and Derby County. Two of these, Oldham and Hull, were opposing each other at Boundary Park and the home side clinched promotion on goal average by winning 3—0.

If Derby County could have won their final game at West Bromwich they would have gone up with Manchester City instead of Oldham, but they were held to a goalless draw with their amateur goalkeeper, H.P. Bailey, giving one of the finest displays of the season. Though suffering from a leg injury, which had caused him to leave the field early on, he resumed and made some remarkable saves while hobbling on one leg and often having to be supported by his team mates.

FOOTBALL FLAVOURED FRAME

CLUES ACROSS:

1 Conquers the opposition
5 Play at Abbey Stadium
11 Terraces cleared — Army way
13 Take over from
15 Take into custody
16 Scottish Clubs Committee (abbrev)
18 The Grecians
19 West Brom's ground
20 The Bees, minus their Ford
21 Rangers stadium
23 Hooliganism has
26 The fans' rosette
28 Dear old Allison
29 Giants' threat to amateurs? (3,3)
33 Troubled, or emphasised
35 Mullery's team in reverse
37 These are The Magpies
38 Cosmos is, in USA

CLUES DOWN:

1 Boundary Park team
2 Yankee in Skelmersdale
3 A young player
4 Goalposts found there
6 Corner! — in church
7 Damage to a shirt
8 Draw up a contract
9 The whole lot
10 Soccer fixture
12 When players come clean (4,5)
14 Sir Stanley Rous was once ---- of F.I.F.A.
16 Noisy protest
17 He lays the odds
22 From August to May
24 A Palace winger?
25 Blown at Upton Park
27 Barrow, minus the nil
30 Singular hunting cry
31 Keegan is to thousands
32 "Get stuck ---- him!"
34 "Blues" second syllable
36 Hearts' first half

ANSWERS ON PAGE 95

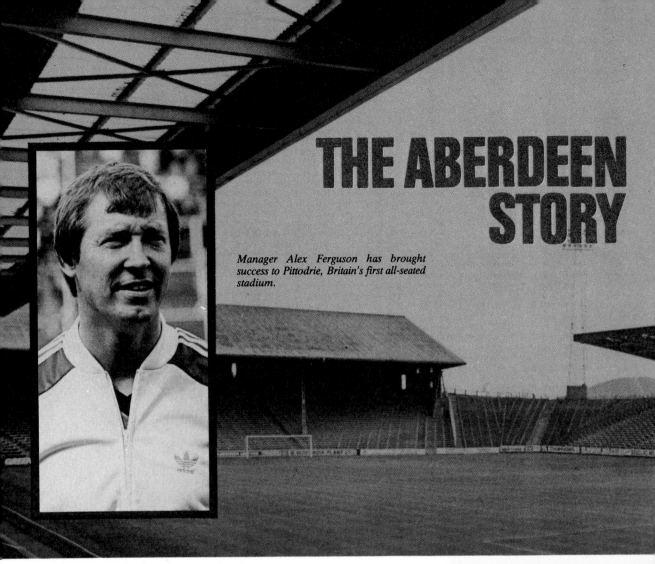

THE ABERDEEN STORY

Manager Alex Ferguson has brought success to Pittodrie, Britain's first all-seated stadium.

ALEX FERGUSON has a burning ambition — to establish Aberdeen as the soccer power in Scotland, to be the equal of the Old Firm giants Celtic and Rangers.

The foundation of that fierce aim was well and truly laid in 1980 when the club won the Championship for the first time in 25 years.

Aberdeen's revival was a long time in coming, but Alex Ferguson will be the first to agree two previous managers made vital contributions to that success.

The much-maligned Ally MacLeod started the ball rolling with the League Cup in 1977.

When "Soccer's Muhammad Ali" left for his brief and controversial spell as Scotland manager, Billy McNeill replaced him.

In McNeill's first season in charge at Pittodrie, The Dons were narrowly beaten 2—1 by Rangers in the Scottish Cup Final and were pipped for the Premier Division title by the Ibrox men.

McNeill left for his old club Celtic when Jock Stein abdicated as laird of Parkhead.

That was when Alex Ferguson, the former Rangers striker and St. Mirren manager, took over.

At the time he said: "There were times when I felt that getting into the Premier Division and staying there was probably good enough for St. Mirren.

"It wasn't for me. Now I have the opportunity to win trophies, to make a mark in the game, because Aberdeen is an important club — and they will remain important.

"They deserve success. Everything is geared for it. I want a squad of players not only capable of reaching the top, but staying there for a long, long time."

Aberdeen are certainly capable of doing that. They also have the perfect setting for continued success: magnificent Pittodrie, Britain's first all-seated soccer stadium.

That's a tremendous achievement in itself for the most Northerly League club in the country.

"We can draw 15,000 fans when we are going reasonably well," says Fergie. "And when Celtic and Rangers

Aberdeen celebrate as Derek McKay scores against Celtic in their 1970 Scottish Cup Final victory over the Glasgow club.

The Dons aim to be masters of Scotland

are here it's always a 24,000 sell-out.''

And few Dons supporters will forget the atmosphere when Liverpool were European Cup-tie visitors last season.

Aberdeen lost the tie but at least they had earned the right to compete with the very best.

Certainly the new-look Pittodrie is a far cry from the Gallows Marsh, a rubbish dump until converted into a football ground back in 1903.

That year three local teams in Aberdeen joined forces. Twelve months later they were elected into the Second Division of the Scottish League.

In May, 1905, the First Division was increased from 14—16 clubs and Aberdeen were voted in.

In 1908, Willie Lennie, who had previously played for Queen's Park, Dundee and Rangers became the club's first real big name star when called up for Scotland.

While The Dons, playing in their famous black and gold stripes, were League Championship runners-up in 1911 and again in 1937, when they

CONTINUED OVER

were also beaten by Celtic in the Scottish Cup Final watched by a massive 146,433 crowd at Hampden, their first major honour didn't arrive until after the War.

That victory in the first-ever Scottish League Cup Final in 1946 was the start of a successful era for Aberdeen, then managed by Davie Halliday.

In the side that beat Rangers 3—2 at Hampden were young Alec Kiddie and George Hamilton, names still remembered at Pittodrie.

A year later Aberdeen won the Scottish Cup for the first time. Even a penalty miss by Hamilton didn't prevent them beating Hibs 2—1 before 82,000 fans.

Eight years later, in 1955, Aberdeen were League Champions. Among their stars at the time were centre-half Alec Young, left-half Archie Glen, goalie Fred Martin and centre-forward Paddy Buckley.

At the start of the following season, Davie Halliday left to take over Leicester City. Trainer David Shaw replaced him and within a few months had taken the club to their second League Cup triumph.

After that victory over St. Mirren it was to be 15 years before another trophy — the Scottish Cup — graced the Pittodrie boardroom.

That was in 1970 . . .the manager Eddie Turnbull.

In the team that shocked the country and Celtic in the Final was Martin Buchan, at 21 the youngest player ever to captain a side in any Scottish Cup Final.

It was local lad Buchan who later moved on to skipper Manchester United to an English Cup Final victory.

Bobby Clark was in goal . . .Boel, Hermiston, G. Murray, McMillan, Robb, Forrest, Harper, Graham and two goal hero Derek Mackay completed Aberdeen's line-up for that memorable afternoon.

But the promised new, eciting era for The Dons never emerged after that. Players left at a furious rate and even

manager Eddie Turnbull was lured to his first love Hibs.

Until the bubbling, irrepressible Ally MacLeod had left Ayr United, the club seemed in danger of sliding to obscurity.

But within a season he had taken them to that extra-time 2—1 League Cup Final win over Celtic and things started to happen.

Soon though, MacLeod moved on to Scotland and disaster in the 1978 World Cup Finals in far away Argentina.

Billy McNeill was MacLeod's successor and he continued the good work despite the fact that the team won nothing while he was there.

Then Alex Ferguson was appointed in charge, dreaming his dreams of glory at home and in Europe.

Young stars Gordon Strachan, Alex McLeish, Willie Miller, Mark McGhee, Andy Watson and Doug Bell are among those capped at various levels for Scotland, a tribute to Ferguson's skilful handling of players as well as the overall running of a top class club.

As Fergie said when Aberdeen clinched the Premier Division title in 1979-80: "This is just the beginning at Pittodrie. There is a lot more to come."

And there will be, make no mistake about that!

ABOVE . . .Alex MacDonald flies through the air to head a goal for Rangers in the 1978 Scottish Cup Final, which Aberdeen lost 2—0. BELOW . . .One of the new heroes of Pittodrie, striker Mark McGhee.

Aston Villa's Gordon Cowans is one of the country's top midfielders. England honours have come his way and he has made a major contribution to Villa's rise over the past year or so.

Yet it was little more than two years ago that Gordon, now 23, was in and out of the Villa team.

"Ron Saunders used to call me in his office and tell me he was resting me. Not dropping me — resting me," remembers the former England Under-21 skipper.

"It was frustrating because I thought I could do a job week after week. When I look back now, though, I realise the boss was right. I wasn't really ready for permanent first-team football."

It was when Andy Gray, John Gidman and John Gregory left Villa that Cowans claimed a regular place. Took on more responsibility.

'NO NERVES NOW'

Says Villa's non-stop midfielder
GORDON COWANS

Gray, who became Britain's most expensive player at £1.5m when he signed for Wolves, has consistently raved about his former team-mate.

"Gordon has everything a top midfielder should have. Pace, skill, power, tackling ability, vision, confidence . . .if he maintains his progress there is no reason why he shouldn't have a long international career," said the Molineux striker.

Cowans has been with Villa since he was 11. Other top clubs such as Arsenal and Manchester City were interested in

him. Despite the fact that Villa were in Division Three, he made his choice.

The player's Mum and Dad used to run a hostel for young players before they moved to the North-East.

It was his dad who gave Gordon his interest in greyhounds. He now co-owns four dogs with his father, with his own greyhound, Barcroft Baron, in the Midlands.

"The prize money is negligible. Fifty pounds if you're lucky, but I like the

involvement and excitement of the meetings. I'm not a heavy gambler — just like to see my dog win."

Cowans, in fact, is very well set up off the field. He owns a large detached house despite being a bachelor and has a rare TR5 sports car, which will gain in value rather than depreciate.

"I won the Robinson's Barley Water Young Player of the Year award and with this came a Rover. I sold that and with the money I bought the TR5."

His "everyday" car is a Ford Capri Ghia supplied by the club. With an income nudging the £1,000 a week mark when Villa are on a winning streak, Cowans is doing very nicely, thank you.

He seems certain to progress with both club and country.

"I'm lucky to play in a Villa side that can express itself. We're an attacking team and this suits my style. Playing for a successful club must boost a player's international chances.

"I used to be very nervous before games. Now, I'm more confident. My size doesn't bother me. I'm 5ft 8ins and under 10 stone, but I can look after myself physically."

Gordon can certainly do that as he ploughs through midfield. Rather like a greyhound at times . . .

91

It may be a dog's life being a footballer, but Gordon isn't complaining!

Brendon in the thick of the action against Southampton.

look changed. I was even made captain. Things started to improve."

Even so, when Atkinson left to take over at West Brom, Batson had no idea that the man nicknamed The Tank as a player would soon come back for the Arsenal reject.

Atki, as he is now known in the Midlands, paid a mere £30,000 for Batson — which wouldn't even cover many signing-on fees today.

"I was given another chance to make a name for myself with a top club," says Brendon. "And I was determined to take it.

"I still have a lot of ambitions to fulfill, but simply playing regularly in what I consider is the best League in the world gives me a lot of satisfaction.

"Naturally I'd like to help Albion win honours and as I'm the right side of 30 I haven't given up all hope of winning an England cap."

Batson is one of those players fans tend to take for granted. He plays so consistently well that he is only noticed when he has a bad game — which is very seldom.

He is reckoned to be one of the snazziest dressers at the club — he's never forgotten the good habits instilled in him at Arsenal. Or how it felt to be discarded as a youngster.

Batson's worked hard for his success . . .and he deserves it.

'Arsenal taught me good habits'

says Albion's Bargain Buy BRENDON BATSON

B rendon Batson is the classic failure who became a success. Now, the Grenada-born player is established as one of the First Division's top full-backs with West Bromwich Albion.

A far cry from the days of the early 70's when after failing to make the grade with Arsenal, he moved to the then new boys of the Football League Cambridge United — and regretted it almost immediately.

"I made half a dozen appearances for Arsenal, standing in for injured players," remembers Brendon. "Don Howe left as coach and Bobby Campbell arrived. I didn't fit into his plans, and I suppose it's true to say I just wasn't good enough for them at the time.

"I still owe Arsenal a lot, though. I picked up a lot of good habits there. The standards are high at Arsenal and Bertie Mee always impressed upon his youngsters that they were representing one of the world's top clubs.

"It may sound silly, but I learnt how to conduct myself in restaurants, how to make sure I never let myself or the

club down."

When it became obvious there was no future for Batson at Highbury he took the plunge and joined League rookies Cambridge United.

"I didn't realise what I'd come into. Too many players lacked ambition, seeming happy just to be playing in the Fourth Division. Then Ron Atkinson took over as manager and everything changed.

"The old players were dropped and younger ones drafted in. The whole club took on a new appearance.

"Mind you, the boss and I didn't always get on. He dropped me because he thought I was becoming complacent, and it was when my wife told me he was right I decided to take a long hard look at myself.

"I trained harder and my whole out-

Ron Atkinson has been a big influence during Brendon's career.

ENGLAND BEAT WORLD CHAMPIONS

March 12th, 1975
ENGLAND 2,
WEST GERMANY 0
at Wembley

SUPERMAC'S FIRST INTERNATIONAL GOAL

After the two most recent World Cup Finals, England took on the winners in friendlies at Wembley — and notched up two memorable wins.

ENGLAND celebrated their 100th appearance at Wembley with a decisive victory over a West Germany side containing five members of the 1974 World Cup winning team.

Don Revie's (above) bold gamble of playing three new caps, Steve Whitworth, Ian Gillard and Alan Hudson, paid off handsomely.

None contributed more to this famous victory than those three rookies, especially Hudson.

Flanked by the experienced Alan Ball and Colin Bell, the Stoke youngster controlled the midfield with the arrogance and skill of an established world class performer.

Brilliant service from Hudson and Bell encouraged Malcolm Macdonald, Kevin Keegan and Mike Channon to push forward at every opportunity.

Even the usually immaculate Franz Beckenbauer and the industrious Bertie Vogts were made to look novices at times as the World Champions struggled to hold the rampaging English lions.

After 25 minutes they took the lead when Hudson's free-kick was hooked into the net by Bell off Cullman.

In the second-half, England tightened their grip, especially when Macdonald scored his first goal at full international level in the 65th minute.

Ball started it with a pass to Channon who pushed the ball on to Bell on the right.

As Bell's centre flew over Maier's head, Macdonald raced forward to head a spectacular goal.

But England weren't finished yet. They ended the match with a flourish ...a shot from Keegan which rebounded off the bar.

England's victory, even against a West Germany side below their best, was still a tremendous achievement.

AFTERMATCH QUOTES

Don Revie (above)
'THIS is the best performance by England since I took over as manager. They proved we have the players in this country who can really play.

Alan Ball did a great job, talking non-stop for 90 minutes.

Hudson did well and has so much natural flair; and like Colin Todd was just out of this world.'

Malcolm Macdonald ploughs his way through the German defence.

ahead. (Right) Argentina are helpless as David Johnson scores his second goal.

AFTERMATCH QUOTES

Helmut Schoen, (left), West Germany manager. 'ENGLAND deserved their win. Our players wanted to play, but some forgot that, before you play, you must win the ball in the tackle.'

Alan Ball, England captain. 'I ENJOYED it, but it wasn't too much different from the job I do for Arsenal.'

THE TEAMS
England: Clemence (Liverpool), Whitworth (Leicester), Watson (Sunderland), Todd (Derby), Gillard (Q.P.R.), Bell (Man. City), Ball (Arsenal), Hudson (Stoke), Channon (Southampton), Macdonald (Newcastle), Keegan (Liverpool). Subs. Shilton (Stoke), Kenyon (Everton), Towers (Sunderland), Thomas (Q.P.R.) and Tueart (Man. City). West Germany: Maier, Bonhof, Vogts, Koerbel, Beckenbauer, Cullmann, Ritschel, Wimmer, Kostedde, Flohe, Holzenbein. Referee: R. Schaut (Belgium).

GREENWOOD'S STARS OUTSHINE SOUTH AMERICAN SUPERMEN

**May 13th, 1980
ENGLAND 3,
ARGENTINA 1
at Wembley.**

ENGLAND thrilled a capacity Wembley crowd with a magnificent win over the 1978 World Champions.

The fans came to see the skills of the South Americans, especially their superstar Diego Maradona, but left enthusing about the form of Dave Watson, Phil Neal, Ray Wilkins, Steve Coppell and the almost unstoppable Kevin Keegan.

Phil Thompson, sweeping up behind his defence, organised operations at the back. And Dave Johnson, a replacement for the badly-injured Trevor Francis, was a revelation.

The game started at a furious pace. Dave Waton's height caused Argentina's defence all sorts of problems as he set up a shot for Kevin Keegan which just scraped the post.

Despite early England pressure Maradona almost put Argentina ahead after a fine, weaving run.

Just as the game seemed to be going the World Champions' way, England took the lead.

Coppell got to the bye-line and centred for Johnson to head past Fillol.

Six minutes into the second-half, the Liverpool star scored again.

His Anfield club-mate Ray Kennedy recovered a pass on the left, beat two defenders and shot for goal.

Fillol could only parry the ball straight to Johnson who tapped it into an empty net.

Argentina came back into the game after 54 minutes through a Passerella penalty, after Kenny Sansom had brought down Maradona.

Urged on by skipper Passerella, the South Americans fought hard for the equaliser, but a tremendous goal by Keegan put the game beyond their reach.

Johnson received the ball from Keegan on the left, passed to Coppell who laid it back for the European Footballer of the Year to beat Fillol with a thunderous drive.

Wembley erupted at the final whistle and the crowd stood to a man to cheer a magnificent game and a memorable England victory.

Argentina's superstar Diego Maradona thrilled the Wembley fans.

AFTERMATCH QUOTES

Diego Maradona. 'ENGLAND played well, especially Kevin Keegan. I've seen him score some great goals on television, but his goal against us proved his class.'

Ron Greenwood. 'ARGENTINA did not come here to defend their World Championship. They were ready to play a game. That is what helped to make it such a great match.
   What a player Maradona is. There is no point trying to mark him so we didn't do so.'

Alberto Tarantini. 'IN all my time with Birmingham I never saw a team play as well as England. They were strong all-round, especially in attack.'

LEFT . . . England captain Kevin Keegan shows the World Champs some of his own tricks. Above . . . Alberto Tarantini, once with Birmingham.

FOOTBALL FLAVOURED FRAME ANSWERS

YOU ARE THE REF ANSWERS

1. Take no action (a). The Laws do not forbid different coloured boots. 2. Time expires when the ball rebounds from the goalkeeper. The goal cannot be allowed (b). 3. Take no action (a). Defenders are not required to remain ten yards away until the ball is played by a second opponent. 4. The incorrect procedure is C. The free-kick must be taken where the ball was when play was stopped (Law 3). In A the free-kick is correctly awarded where the player was when play was stopped (Law 12). In B the players are correctly cautioned when the ball is out of play (Law 3).

FOR THESE SHOWBIZ STARS-
SOCCER'S TOP OF THE POPS

ABOVE . . .Watford chairman Elton John with Eric and Ernie. Elton's the one with the short fat hairy leg!

RIGHT . . .Pop superstar Rod Stewart would love to play for Scotland at Hampden Park.

THE £100,000 "flop" was left in no doubt what was expected of him . . .

Simply, he had to fill the boots of a player who had just left the club for almost £1 million!

That was the task that fell to Aberdeen's Mark McGhee last season after the Pittodrie club had sold master marksman Steve Archibald to Spurs. McGhee, who cost The Dons £60,000 after failing to make the grade with Newcastle following his £100,000 transfer from Morton, accepted the role without argument.

Today fans and rival defenders alike are absolutely baffled as to why Newcastle didn't give super striker McGhee a proper chance to show his ability at St. James's Park.

McGhee failed to last a season with Newcastle and says: "The team were in trouble when I joined them and there was a lot of pressure all over the place.

"I was in at the start and then out again. There was no consistent place for me and I felt like a bit of a stranger at times. Eventually, I was happy to go home to Scotland again.

"When I heard Aberdeen had offered £60,000 for me I couldn't get across that Border quickly enough. I never lost faith in my ability although, of course, my confidence took a bit of a dent."

Actually, McGhee's spell with Newcastle was his second bid at making the grade in England. He went to Bristol City as a teenager, but says: "I felt terribly homesick at the time and asked for my release. Thankfully, they allowed me to leave on a free transfer."

Celtic were interested in the fleet-footed McGhee, who was then operating as an outside-right with the flair for scoring goals from uncanny angles.

MARK McGHEE— IN THE BIG-TIME AT LAST

During his managership of Celtic, Jock Stein — now Scotland boss — was interested in signing the fleet-footed McGhee.

Jock Stein was impressed, but before he could finalise any deal he was involved in his unfortunate car accident seven years ago and McGhee drifted out of sight.

Morton, though, moved in swiftly after offering him a trial and he rebuilt his career and his reputation at Cappielow before trying again in England with Newcastle.

Today, Mark McGhee is a wiser footballer for all his travels and experiences and he says: "Just being with Aberdeen makes up for anything that might have gone in the past.

"When we won the Premier League title to become the first club outside the Old Firm of Celtic and Rangers to win it in 15 years the feeling was difficult to describe. We fought all the way and in the end no one begrudged us our victory. I think even Celtic fans agreed we were the best team in Scotland!"

McGhee has taken over where Steve Archibald left off, scoring goals with a flourish and no little panache. He may have taken a strange route to get to the top, but now he has arrived he intends staying there for a long, long time to come.

'I wish would

E VEN though it will make my job as a defender much more difficult, I'd welcome a return of the wingers.

Sadly until managers and coaches remove some of the fear from football and are prepared to take risks I can't see wingers making a big comeback.

Managers are terrified of losing games — and their jobs. These days of 4-3-3 wingers are a luxury teams can't afford because they rely on service from midfield. Without a regular supply of balls, wingers can be out of a game for long periods.

In today's game the old-fashioned winger has been replaced by what we call "wide men", players like Steve Coppell of Manchester United. He is expected to drop back when necessary and tackle opponents, act as an extra full-back.

Probably the only two "real" wingers still in the First Division are Peter Barnes and John Robertson.

Peter, discarded by Manchester City and then England, took a while to establish himself at West Brom.

He still lacks consistency, but on his day Peter can destroy teams on his own, a real match-winner whose style excites the fans.

Forest winger John Robertson (dark shirt) has the ability to beat a man and leave him completely off balance.

Wingers fly again'

given his freedom by manager Ron Atkinson.

Big Ron didn't buy Peter as a midfielder or extra defender. He wanted him to produce things on the flanks.

It amazes me why more managers don't go for wingers. The best way to beat a defence is to go round the fullback, reach the bye-line and pull the ball back into the goal-mouth.

There's no finer sight in football than a winger going down the flank, beating his full-back on the outside with a swerve of the body or flick of the foot.

Another reason I suppose managers don't use wingers is ... they are in short supply.

If we had a few more Peter Barnes' and John Robertsons' in the game gates would soar.

John has certainly provided the Nottingham Forest fans with many thrills over the past few years.

Leighton James (above) tore England to shreds at Wrexham. Peter Barnes (left) has been given the freedom of West Brom.

Robbo has the ability to beat a man and leave him completely off balance with no chance of recovery. He can also score goals and take penalty kicks!

Brian Clough and Peter Taylor are responsible for John's success as a winger, recognising you get nothing for sitting back and not taking chances.

Leighton James is an out-and-out winger still turning on the magic.

The Welsh international found a new lease of life at Swansea after a career spanning Burnley (twice), Derby County and Q.P.R.

I remember seeing him tear England to shreds in the 1980 British Championship at Wrexham. Wingers a luxury?

CONTINUED OVER

Not if Leighton James is anything to go by.

The tactics devised by Alf Ramsey back in the Sixties really killed off wing men. He believed their role would be better filled by an inside-forward going wide, or an overlapping full-back.

Ramsey's thinking certainly brought results. England won the World Cup and clubs all over the world copied their style.

Suddenly all the kids wanted to be Geoff Hursts or Bobby Charltons. Now it's Trevor Brooking, or Trevor Francis. No one wants to be another Stan Matthews, Tom Finney or George Best.

Mind you, I suppose we did enjoy a mini-revival during the late Sixties and mid-Seventies.

Liverpool had the dazzling pair Phil Thompson and Steve Heighway ... Burnley John Connolly ... Southampton Terry Paine ... Leeds Eddie Gray and Manchester United Gordon Hill.

Gordon left Old Trafford soon after I arrived even though he was idolised by the fans. He could beat players and scored at least 14 goals a season, but he didn't fit in with Dave Sexton's plans for the future of United.

He went off to Derby where a serious injury prevented his career getting off the ground. Gordon was transferred to Q.P.R. when Tommy Docherty took over but hardly kicked a ball for them.

Hilly is in Canada, now, playing for Montreal. What a waste of talent.

I've always had a soft spot for wingers because that's where I started out as a 16-year-old playing for St. Mirren Boys Guild.

There's no finer sight than a winger in full flight ... Top: Steve Heighway in the 1974 F.A. Cup Final. Above: Gordon Hill, a sad waste of talent. Below: Celtic's Jimmy Johnstone, one of the greatest of them all.

I enjoyed the role and had a reasonable amount of success — until I began to mature physically.

I grew and grew, put on a bit of beef and was spotted by a scout for Scottish junior club Largs Thistle.

He offered me a trial with the club provided I turned out at centre-half!

Naturally I was prepared to play anywhere as Largs were a respected club in Ayrshire.

Fortunately I adapted to the switch very easily and haven't looked back.

I went on to St. Mirren and played against two of the finest wingmen of all time — Celtic's Jimmy Johnstone and Willie Henderson of Rangers.

Jinky and Wee Willie were so good, provided such a wide range of skills, they were like a couple of circus acts.

If only they were around today clubs wouldn't have a problem finding enough fans to fill their terraces. They'd have trouble keeping them out!

I'd try to use wingers if I ever become a manager. But it's easy to make that sort of promise when my job isn't on the line.

Perhaps one day the directors will relieve the pressure on managers and allow them more freedom, to bring back some of the fun to football.

Gordon McQueen

GARY SHAW
Aston Villa

Brian Clough. Malcolm Allison. Tommy Docherty. Lawrie McMenemy . . . These days managers rapidly become household names and get more headlines than their players. Did managers in the old days get the same blaze of publicity? Or is it a modern phenomenon?

For example, does the name Miguel Muñoz ring a bell?

In case it doesn't, he was a member of the superb, attacking Real Madrid side that dominated European football in the late 50s. As their skipper, he was the first man to lift the European Cup in triumph, and he went on to become manager of Real for a record-breaking 14 years of unparalleled successes.

Nowadays Miguel Muñoz is still a top First Division manager in Spain and, in an exclusive interview with SHOOT Annual he tries to explain how football and football management have changed in the years since Real Madrid sensationally scooped up every trophy in sight,

How the game has changed

"You're right, managers seem to be given a lot more importance these days — though I think it's more accurate to say that we're over-publicised. Because I think the media have changed their approach to football. I mean Real Madrid were always in the news, but people talked about our *football*. In the last 20 years there's been a certain . . . er . . . decadence, for want of a better word, in the way the Press treat the game. They prefer to talk about things *related* to football rather than the football itself. They seem to enjoy paddling around in the gravy, and forget about the meat.

"Having said that, there was another factor at work with the great Real Madrid side. When you have a team of superbly gifted stars the media have more names to choose from, and the manager stays tucked away further in the background. To give you another example, a lot of people couldn't tell you the name of the manager of the 1970 Brazil side, even though Pelé, Rivelino, Jairzinho, Gerson and the rest have gone down in the history of the game.

"Football itself has certainly changed a fair amount since the Real Madrid days. In fact, it's changing imperceptibly all the time, but you don't notice all the changes when you're closely involved in the game. Basically, everything has improved. Maybe not so much in ball skills, but physical preparation is a lot better these days, and tactically the game has developed a great deal. And I

don't just mean playing with numbers, like 4-3-3 or 4-4-2. I suppose these 'systems' are innovations compared with the old concept of wing-halves and inside-forwards, but let's not deceive ourselves by thinking of these as important changes. Because in my view, the most important change in football has been the development of the 'all-rounder'. In the Real Madrid days football was still basically a static game, with the winger sticking to his wing and defenders sticking to defence. Everyone played more or less according to his position on the team-sheet.

"Nowadays players are infinitely more flexible with regard to their position on the field. Defenders are expected to lend a hand in attack. Attackers are expected to mark opponents when the other team has the ball. Everybody is more mobile, and all the players have a more active role in the game. The days of a winger patrolling his touchline for half an hour without touching the ball are finished. The modern player has to be able to perform in practically any position on the field.

"As for management, I feel that basically the job hasn't changed all that much, even though we're brought

much more to the public's notice these days. Speaking personally, life was much more hectic for me at Real than it has been recently with more modest teams. But the idea is the same everywhere — to produce a balanced and effective team with confidence and morale. This will never change.

"People say that Real must have been a difficult side to handle, because there were so many big names in the team. But I didn't have any big problems. Or little ones either! And this is something that hasn't changed in football. Real were a happy group of people. A happy team. And if we hadn't formed such a happy group, I don't believe we would have won all the titles we did. This is something that has always been true in football, and always will be.

"Some people maintain that fear of losing is killing football as a spectacle. Hmmm . . . maybe defensive tactics have become more sophisticated, but I don't know that this has changed as much as people think. At Real we were sometimes afraid of losing, I must admit — and this was the most difficult part of being their manager. Everyone expected us to win *every* game, and sometimes the whole team really felt tremendous psychological pressure because of this.

"What's more, we were not only expected to win — we were expected to win with sensational football. Fortunately, with men like di Stéfano, Puskas, Kopa, Gento, Santamaría and so on in

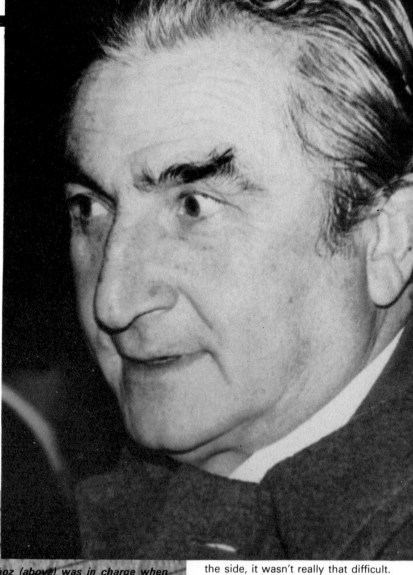

Muñoz (above) was in charge when Real beat Eintracht Frankfurt 7—3 at Hampden Park. Here Puskas nets a penalty.

the side, it wasn't really that difficult. That's one thing I notice about football these days — there's a world shortage of teams like Real, who won matches with attractive attacking football. But nowadays it's difficult for one club to bring together top world talents as Real did. A team like that *guaranteed* spectacular soccer, because there was so much talent in the side. Now there are very few players in the world who can provide inspired football — especially now that personalities like Cruyff have disappeared from the international scene.

"You say Menotti's Argentina team are playing the most attractive football these days? Hmmm . . . I think there's certainly a lot of entertaining football played in the Argentine leagues. But, you know, I wonder how Argentina will play in the next World Cup. Menotti's been lucky with results so far, but I wonder if they'll carry on playing attractive stuff if they kick off with a bad result? Everyone would like to play entertaining football, but you've got to keep one eye on the scoreboard.

"Being so closely involved with that great Real team is an experience that has influenced me a lot. Subconsciously I suppose I'm always aiming to produce

103

CONTINUED OVER

another side with the same ability, even though I'm well aware of the different set of priorities in more modest clubs. The Brazilians are having terrible problems in forgetting their great side of 1970, and can't seem to reconcile themselves to accepting less talented teams. But until they do, they won't get anywhere. By the same token, I wouldn't have got anywhere as a manager if I hadn't realised that not every team can be as good as Real Madrid.

"None of us complained about the money we were earning with Real, but today's footballers get an awful lot more — even taking into account the cost of living and all the rest of it. I don't think that today's big money is either good or bad for the game. A real footballer enjoys the game and gives it all he's got, whether he's earning big money or little money.

"You ask me whether I think the great Real Madrid side would be a good side in today's game . . . Well, my answer is 'no'. They wouldn't be a good team. They'd be a great team. Without a shadow of a doubt. If those superb players of 20 years ago had today's physical preparation and tactical awareness, they'd be world-beaters. Football may have evolved and developed, but you'll never find a substitute for sheer skill . . ."

Personalities such as Johan Cruyff have disappeared.

QUICK-WORD

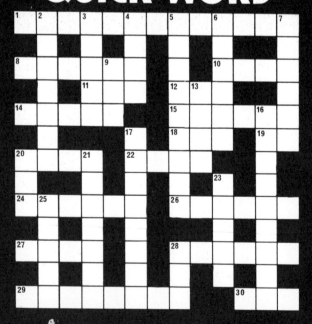

ACROSS

1 Dutch international, veteran of 1974 and 1978 World Cups, currently playing with Cosmos
8 Home park of a Welsh club
10 . . .er . . .well . . .this could be the start of a famous Scottish club
11 Number of subs permitted in Football League games
12 If you want to get ahead, get an international . . .
14 Upright supporter (1 and 4)
15 Surprise qualifiers for the European Championship Finals
18 A chunk from the centre of Liverpool's boss
19 It's an advantage if the ref waves play this way
20 Christian name of Austrian striker sounds like appeal for handball
22 The crowd shouts "oooooooh" when the ball does this to 14 across
24 Nickname of much-travelled defender who achieved his major honours with Chelsea, now Bournemouth coach
26 Arsenal player seemingly destined for distinguished England international career
27 Frank O'Farrell did some of the early groundwork in this country, who pulled off a surprise result in the last World Cup
28 Frans Thijssen's old club
29 Flamengo and former Brazil boss for 1978 World Cup
30 Blond Scots defender who hit fame with Arsenal. Ian . . .

DOWN

2 South American Champions in 1979, but Forest refused to meet this team to contest the Intercontinental Cup
3 What the Spaniards will say to the World Cup on July 11th, 1982
4 Portugal's top scorer at international level in recent years
5 Ipswich striker with an open-and-shut name (4 and 5)
6 Argentinian christened "El Matador" after his World Cup performance
7 Man who led West Germany to the world title in 1974
9 After success in recent seasons the mood of Forest fans has been triumph . . .
13 Name shared by Greek side based in Salonica and last year's Luxembourg Cup-winners from Bonnevoie
16 Cruyff's businessman father-in-law who master-minded Johan's and other players' careers (3 and 6)
17 The man who scored England's first goal in the 1966 World Cup
20 The first slice off The Blades' boss Harry . . .lam
21 Runs from posts to stanchions (4 and 3)
23 European Cup winners beaten by Celtic in the 1967 Final
25 Mickey Walsh joined them in 1980
28 Number of goals scored by 6 down against Poland in the 1978 World Cup

'A RANGERS FAN –
but I'll do them no favours on the pitch'

says Alex MacDonald of Hearts

"I 'LL always be a Rangers fan. I'm a season ticket-holder and I'll be keeping it that way. Whenever I stop playing you'll find me on the terraces roaring on the lads . . ."

There's nothing so unusual about those words. Rangers, after all, are one of the best supported clubs in the game with fans dotted all over the world.

However, those words were being said by a player who was LEAVING Rangers that day to join another club!

Last season brought the sad departure of Alex MacDonald from Ibrox as he took his considerable and combative midfield skills to Hearts.

"It had to happen one day," says MacDonald. "There's no point in looking back. I will give everything for Hearts, but, of course, I will never be able to disguise my feelings for Rangers.

"The years I had there were simply marvellous. They are memories that will live with me forever. My future, though, is with Hearts. I'll give them every ounce of energy I possess."

Proving the 100 per cent professional outlook of MacDonald, who won one full Scottish international cap against Switzerland six years ago, some of his most memorable displays have been AGAINST Rangers.

"They'll get my backing off the pitch, but they can expect no favours when we're in opposition," says MacDonald. "That's not my style. It never has been and never will be."

MacDonald even had the Rangers applauding a goal he netted against their favourites last season when he worked a one-two through the heart of the rearguard and left goalkeeper Peter McCloy helpless with a whiplash shot of unerring accuracy.

Hearts eventually lost that game 3—1, but they managed a goalless draw in the next encounter and MacDonald was undoubtedly the man of the afternoon as he patrolled and controlled the middle of the park.

"I feel as fit as when I started my career with St. Johnstone," says MacDonald. "I look after myself and keep myself in condition. My future? I'll take every game as it comes. You can't really plan too far ahead in this game.

"Injuries can take their toll, but thankfully I have never been particularly injury prone."

MacDonald is a typical Scottish terrier of a player much in the mould of Archie Gemmill and Asa Hartford. He battles for everything, chasing loose balls and always keeping the pressure on opponents.

The game needs honest professionals such as Alex MacDonald. He rarely gets the credit he so richly deserves, but rival players are always swift to tell you just how much he means to his club.

"That's enough for me," says Mighty Mac.

SOCCER TOP

Showbiz people and those whose stage is grass, the professional footballers, have always shared a close affinity bordering on a love affair.

Stage comedians, in particular, enjoy a warm relationship with players, "dining out" on soccer stories whenever the spotlights are trained on them.

What would Tommy Trinder have done for gags without his beloved Fulham, of which he is now Life President? The Craven Cottage club has become as much a part of Tommy's act as West Ham has "Alf Garnett's".

One of Tommy's favourite yarns was the tale of Billy Walker's hat-trick of penalties in a League game. He did it for Aston Villa against Bradford City whose goalkeeper was a fiery Scot named Jock Ewart.

Walker had scored twice when the third penalty was given. Tommy takes up the story: "Walker took it and sent the ball wide. The referee ruled that a Bradford player had moved. Walker got a second crack. This time he sent it over the bar.

"Again the referee ordered the kick to be retaken on the grounds that a player had moved into the box.

"This was too much for Ewart. While Walker rolled the ball into an unguarded net, Ewart leaned against his post, shouting to the ref, 'There you are. Satisfied now? He's got his ruddy hat-trick!'"

Mike Yarwood is as much in love with football as he is with "silly Billy" Denis Healey and the other personalities he impersonates.

Mike's soccer passion is centred on Stockport County, a Lancashire club he has supported for more than 25 years.

"The crowds are not big at Stockport," grins Mike. "I stood on the terraces once, fag in mouth, and had to walk 200 yards to get a light."

He also claims hilariously that 200 policemen lined-up outside the Stockport ground at home games, throwing the hooligans *in* to swell the gate.

West Ham's preparation for a game at Leeds was interrupted by an invitation from Mike and Bernie Winters, lifelong Hammers supporters, to occupy a row of the theatre they were playing at Bradford.

Unfortunately, poor Bernie was knocked unconscious during the show by a lump of metal hurled from the audience. As they carried the big man off stage, the comedian overheard Bobby Moore remark: "If that's show business, give me football anytime."

Barbara Windsor, bosomy star of the "Carry On" films, has long admired Arsenal Football Club. Frank McLintock used to be her favourite in the famous "double" days, but a more regular visitor to Highbury is Pete Murray, radio's popular disc jockey.

Little and Large, another comic double act, definitely did not see the funny side of Manchester City's demise under Malcolm Allison before his resignation in the autumn of 1980.

"It was terrible," says Eddie Large. "I kept hearing Bernard Manning, George Roper and other comics taking the mickey out of City, and I couldn't bear to listen. Not because they weren't good jokes, but because it was MY team they were referring to."

John Bond's arrival as Manager at Maine Road swept a smile back on to Eddie's face — and the jokes began to flow again.

"He's great that John Bond. I like his brother, Premium. And his other brother James is okay, given the 007

shirt for a berth on the right wing."

It wasn't the Little and Large team who cracked the joke about Malcolm Allison breaking into a cigarette machine — looking for 10 players!

Eddie: "Manchester United are on the telly next week."

Syd: "What programme's that, Eddie?"

Eddie: "Survival!"

OF THEIR POPS

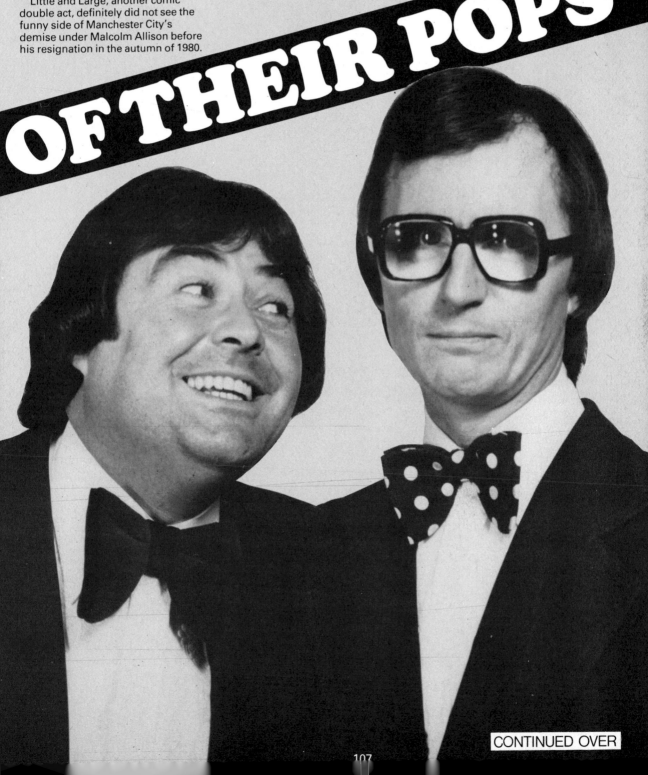

CONTINUED OVER

Kimberley Santos, the 1980-81 Miss World, confesses she would love to manage a Football League side, preferably Arsenal.

"I know it sounds crazy, but I've already got some of the qualifications," (A 36-24-36 formation?) she said, dashing across the tarmac at Heathrow to another assignment during her year of office.

"I managed my high school team in Guam. I can play the game and I am studying sports medicine. I'd love to be manager of Arsenal." Watch out Terry Neill, she's prettier than you!

Jasper Carrott has pledged his support for Birmingham City, rarely missing a home game at St. Andrews and following the team on many of their excursions away from the city.

Jasper, star of television and stage, recalls the moment Gary Pendrey of Birmingham committed a late tackle.

"Pendrey looked amazed when the referee called him over for a lecture. 'What's up, ref?' he enquired. 'That was a very late tackle, son' came the reply. 'But I got there as fast as I could, ref . . .'"

Stewpot's "Header"

Where would Everton be without Ed Stewart's blessing? "Stewpot" idolises the Goodison Park club and stars such as Mick Lyons, Mick McMahon, Eamonn O'Keefe and John Bailey.

He would like to play football for Everton as well as entertain his millions of young listeners on the radio.

"Stewpot" was working on the pirate ship, Radio London, when Everton met Sheffield Wednesday in the 1966 F.A. Cup Final. He was given permission to record the middle hour of his afternoon programme so that he could watch the big game on television.

"When Derek Temple scored the winner," recalls Ed, "I jumped up in excitement, completely forgetting I was on an old wartime minesweeper, and struck my head on the low bulkhead.

"When they brought me round 15 minutes later, they told me that Everton had won. My head was so painful it felt I had headed the winner."

Elton John, Ben Warriss of Jewel and Warriss fame, David Hamilton, Bernard Manning . . . soccer has many friends in the entertainment world.

One comedian who fell out of love with the game and promises never to support it again is Bernard Cribbins.

He was persuaded to play soccer when he was in the army. He took a full-blooded drive in his private parts in the one and only game he has played.

"Down I went. They helped me off the field, I took no further part in the game and wasn't asked to play again."

Who knows, he might have become as good as Trevor Francis . . . given time!

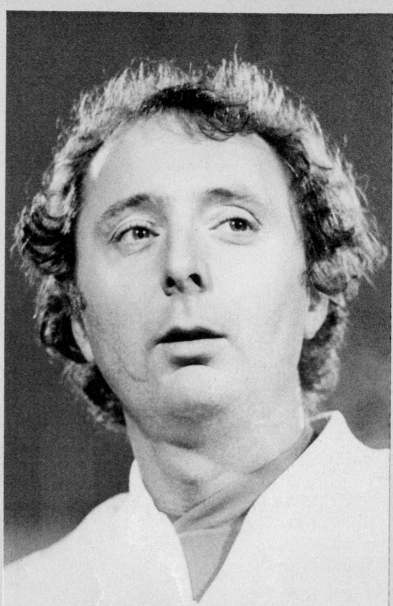

MAIN PICTURE
Jasper Carrot is a director of Birmingham City.
BELOW
BBC disc jockey Pete Murray is often seen at Highbury.

1979 . . . United beat Aberdeen in the Bell's League Cup Final replay 3—0. Manager Jim McLean and captain Paul Hegarty display the Cup to jubilant Tannadice fans.

TWO-IN-A-ROW FOR DUNDEE UNITED

1980 . . . United defeat neighbours Dundee 3—0 at Dens Park. Here are two of United's goals, both scored by Paul Sturrock.

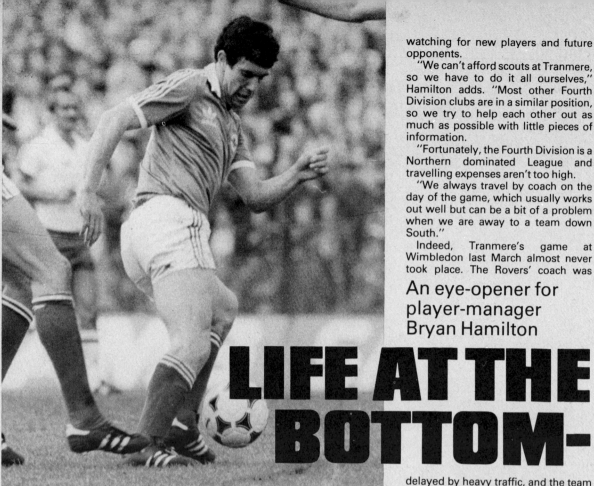

watching for new players and future opponents.

"We can't afford scouts at Tranmere, so we have to do it all ourselves," Hamilton adds. "Most other Fourth Division clubs are in a similar position, so we try to help each other out as much as possible with little pieces of information.

"Fortunately, the Fourth Division is a Northern dominated League and travelling expenses aren't too high.

"We always travel by coach on the day of the game, which usually works out well but can be a bit of a problem when we are away to a team down South."

Indeed, Tranmere's game at Wimbledon last March almost never took place. The Rovers' coach was

An eye-opener for player-manager Bryan Hamilton

LIFE AT THE BOTTOM-

AFTER more than 15 years at the top as an international footballer, Bryan Hamilton has gone to the foot of the ladder in his new career as soccer manager.

Hamilton, the likeable Ulsterman who gained 50 full caps for Northern Ireland during a career which took in such glamorous names as Ipswich and Everton, was appointed manager of Fourth Division Tranmere Rovers in September, 1980.

And he is the first to admit that life at the wrong end of the Football League has proved something of an eye-opener.

"Our biggest headache is over training facilities," he explains. "We don't have anywhere of our own, so we have to hire a pitch from the local council.

"That isn't such a bad arrangement, but when it rains we are in trouble. We can't risk messing up the pitch, because we don't want to upset the local authorities.

"Often it's a case of all the players driving around the area until we can find a suitable bit of space to train on.

"We don't have a gymnasium, either, so we have to rely on local schools and youth clubs for the loan of their facilities."

As player-manager at Prenton Park, Hamilton gets precious little spare time these days. In his first four months at Tranmere he clocked up 20,000 miles in his car, driving all over the country

ABOVE . . .Tranmere boss Bryan Hamilton on the ball.
BELOW . . .John Kelly has done well for Rovers.

delayed by heavy traffic, and the team reached Plough Lane just ten minutes before kick-off.

The League fined Rovers for that late arrival, an expense the little Merseyside club could well have done without.

"Obviously we can't expect top players to come to Rovers on our wages, so we concentrate on signing youngsters and free transfer players looking for first-team football," Hamilton continued.

"Often we spot a good young lad, but he isn't interested in joining a little club like ours. At that age they naturally want the best.

"All I can tell them is that they will get the chance to progress and develop much quicker here than at most clubs.

"Apprentices train with the first team on their first day at the club, and we can throw players into the League side much earlier.

"I am fortunate in that I have some good players here at Tranmere. But most of the lads don't realise just how good they are, and my job is to convince them we can do better.

"Finances dictate so much here. Jim Lumby was doing a great job in our attack, but as soon as Mansfield came in with a £50,000 bid, I had to accept. Fortunately young John Kelly has filled his place well, and he is going to be worth quite a bit to this club in the near future.

"I'm sure that starting at the bottom is the only way to learn soccer management, but I don't intend to stay in that position for ever.

Spurs have sharpened Steve

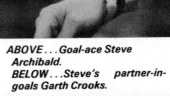

S PURS striker Steve Archibald is convinced that he is a better player for his £800,000 transfer from Scotland's leading club Aberdeen.

The Scottish international who netted more than 20 goals in his first seven months at White Hart Lane has solved an acute scoring problem at Tottenham.

And as the blond-haired Glaswegian admits: "My finishing is better than at any other stage in my career.

"I feel so much sharper since my move from Pittodrie, and my left foot has improved to such an extent that I am now equally confident with either foot."

Yet Archibald reckons that such improvements in front of goal have only come at the expense of his team-work.

"I now concentrate solely on taking up scoring positions," he confesses. "My only concern now is putting the ball away, and this has meant my general team play has inevitably suffered.

"But I was bought by Spurs to score goals, and I reckon that as long as I am doing that nobody is going to complain."

Archibald has been helped in his quest for goals by his striking partner

ABOVE . . . Goal-ace Steve Archibald.
BELOW . . . Steve's partner-in-goals Garth Crooks.

Garth Crooks, and the Scotsman is quick to acknowledge the value of his team-mate's contribution.

Yet he reserves his greatest admiration for midfield maestro Glenn Hoddle. "When I was at Aberdeen I didn't rate Glenn all that highly," Archibald says. "But now I know differently.

" I have never played with a more skilful footballer before. His distribution is unbelievable, and I just cannot understand how Glenn isn't a regular in the England team. I only wish he was eligible for Scotland."

When Archibald arrived at Spurs at the beginning of the 1980-81 season, however, he anticipated a few problems with Hoddle, Ardiles and the other members of the Spurs midfield.

"Last season Glenn and Ossie seemed to use the forwards as a wall just to get the ball back as quickly as possible.

"Glenn scored a lot of goals, so naturally he kept playing this way.

"But Garth and I told them we wouldn't play to that system. We wanted a quick, killer ball played to our feet for Garth and myself to have a go for goal.

"So far it's worked like a dream."

SPOT THE DIFFERENCE

Compare the two sketches to find the 12 alterations that have been made by our artist to the bottom one. They are printed upside-down below.

112

"WHY HAMPDEN IS SPECIAL TO ME"

HAMPDEN PARK. Those two words mean Scottish football to me . . .

It's been called "The White Elephant" of Scottish football for a long time and it would never be rated in the class of, say, The Maracana in Brazil, but for legions of Scottish football fans over the years it has been the home of golden, treasured memories, heart-stopping moments, uncontrolled joy and, of course, agony and grief if things haven't gone quite according to plan!

I'm a firm believer in always looking forward in the game, but I would like to linger on some of the memories that make Hampden so special to me.

I was born and brought up in Dundee and I can always remember the day Scotland would play at Hampden and my brothers and I used to crowd round the television set when it was on 'live'. Our friends came in, too, and what a din we could make.

Hampden roar? You should have been in the Johnstone household in Dundee. We always seemed to make more noise than anyone else at the actual game!

I remember when Alan Gilzean headed in the only goal of the game in 1964 and I was caught with mixed emotions. I was delighted, of course, that Alan had scored and my country had beaten the Auld Enemy again, but Alan was a Dundee player at the time and I was a Dundee United supporter.

Dundee's not that big, you know, and a lot of my friends were Dundee fans. They kept telling me I should support a good team with some good players and that United were a load of old rubbish. When Alan was later transferred to Spurs it cut them short in their tracks.

By the way, I really did admire Alan's ability in the air when I was a kid, and I suppose the prowess with his head in the penalty box might have rubbed off on to a young Derek Johnstone. I'll tell you one thing . . . I wouldn't mind scoring the winning goal against England anywhere.

But to get back to Hampden. I'll always remember that astonishing ten-goal European Cup Final classic in Glasgow when Real Madrid took seven off West Germany's Eintracht Frankfurt in 1960.

Eintracht were a very good team at the time — they knocked out Rangers in the tourney beating them home and away — and that adds to the feat of Puskas, di Stefano and Ghento. They were magnificent.

The name of Hampden proudly stands alongside all that is good in football. When I first played there as a 16-year-old I could hardly believe my luck.

It's history now that I played against Celtic in the 1970 League Cup Final years ago, scoring the only goal of the game. I remember that match for two things. I didn't actually see my dream goal go into the net. I was twisting and turning away after getting my head to a right wing cross from Willie Johnston to send the ball away from goalkeeper Evan Williams.

So I never saw the most important goal in my career, the goal that started it all for yours truly. The other thing I remember distinctly was the mighty roar that went up from one end of the ground while the other was in total silence.

It was a strange feeling. Out there on the pitch you are in the middle of things and watching one end of a ground leap around and send scarves into the air while the other stays stock still is quite astounding. I don't mind it too much just so long as it's the Rangers fans who are celebrating and singing!

I've scored a few goals at good old Hampden for my club and country and that's why I was so sad to read and hear last year the National Stadium was in danger.

Hampden will always have a special place in my heart . . .

One of Derek's golden memories is of scoring Rangers' only and winning goal in the 1970 League Cup Final against Celtic.

TONY
CURRIE
Q.P.R.

**ALAN
YOUNG**
Leicester
City

Laugh in the New Year

"The coming year seems to hold connections with the army — I keep getting 'marching orders'."

"You'd win first prize for originality if you go as a footballer."

"I got the boys to pin up their New Year's resolutions, boss..."

NEVER ARGUE WITH THE REF - EVEN WHEN HE'S RIGHT SIGNED Butch

NEVER COMMIT A PROFESSIONAL FOUL IN AN UNPROFESSIONAL MANNER SIGNED Richard

TO ALWAYS GIVE MY BEST - PROVIDING THE MONEY IS RIGHT SIGNED Charlie

NEVER TO RAISE MY TWO FINGERS BEHIND MY MANAGERS BACK SIGNED Jock

KEEP MY TEMPER WHEN THE FANS GIVE ME STICK - BLOW 'EM A RAZZBERRY INSTEAD - SIGNED Joe

"Before I take this vital last-minute penalty, I'd just like to wish you a Happy New Year."

"But tell me, my dear, what is it your husband is supposed to be?"

"Remember the resolutions you made last year, boss? We were going to win the Cup, the League and crush Europe . . ."

"What a fantastic start to the New Year — we only lost by three goals!"

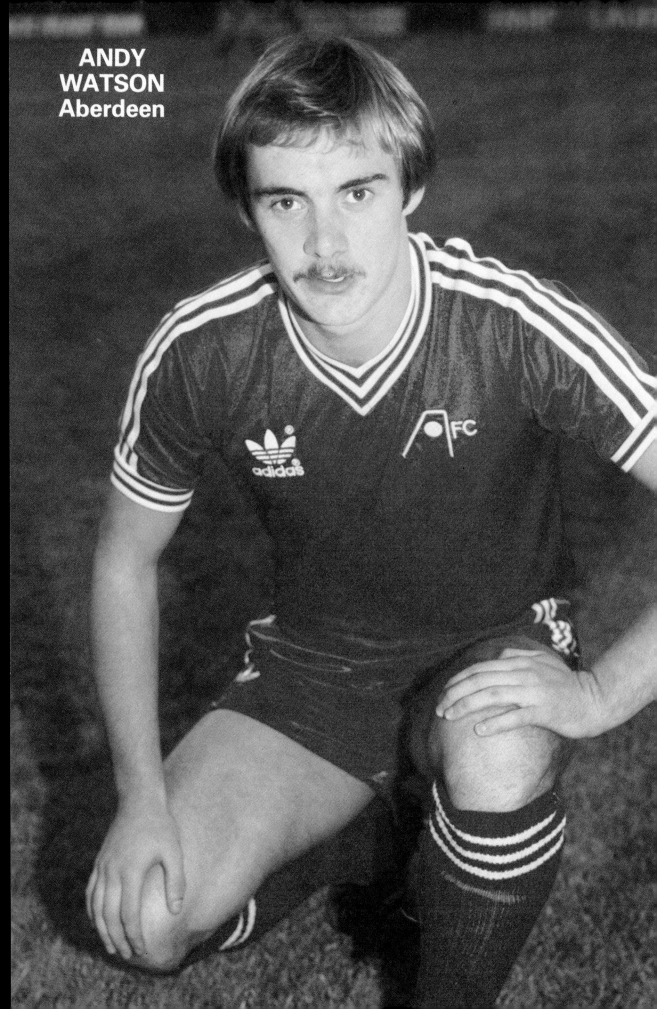

ANDY
WATSON
Aberdeen

**FRANK
WORTHINGTON**
Birmingham
City

What would you think if you saw a player in a League match racing down the field under an umbrella? But that's not fantasy, it's fact. Many years ago Aston Villa were playing Sheffield United in a First Division game when a terrific rainstorm burst over the ground. Soon the players were soaked and the pitch turned into a quagmire. After a few minutes a fan offered an umbrella to Charlie Athersmith, Villa's famous England international right winger. Charlie accepted it gratefully and off he went down the wing holding the umbrella over his dripping head. Not to be outdone his attacking partner, John Devey, also a much-capped England star, borrowed a long raincoat from a fan and while the downpour lasted the two Villa team-mates were able to continue playing with some protection. The fans roared with approval and even the referee had to admire the audacity of the "undercover" Villans.

That incident could not happen in modern football but years ago nearly every team had its crowd-pleasing personality. One of the greatest — in size as well as popularity — was Billy Foulke, nicknamed Fatty. He was certainly a giant, standing 6ft. 3in. and weighing over 22 stone, but his unorthodox goalkeeping and sense of humour were as big as his stature. No wonder the fans loved him. During his long service with Sheffield United he would think nothing of carrying two of his team-mates, both under 5ft. 6in., on to the field to roars of applause from the fans. On one occasion a Liverpool forward had the audacity to charge him after he had made a save, so Billy grabbed the offender by his legs and stood him on his head in the goal-mouth. All in fun, of course!

Entertaining

Fatty Foulke later joined Chelsea and was appointed their first captain. But his light-hearted approach to the game never changed. To call attention to his vast bulk Chelsea used to send him on to the field carrying two small boys, in club colours. He would ceremoniously place one of the boys on each side of his goal to act as ball-boys. Just before the start of one League game the referee drew Billy's attention to the fact that he was wearing a shirt the same colour as the opposition and must change.

Off went the huge goalie and soon returned to the field wearing a large white bath towel wrapped around his ample figure. He apologised to the ref saying that he could not find an alternative shirt to fit him — hence the towel. Perhaps it was true but even the ref knew better than to argue with the amiable giant.

A whole book could be written about the great goalkeeper personalities of the past, Albert Iremonger among them. He stood around 6ft. 5in. and played in over 600 League and Cup

games for Notts County. Lanky Albert certainly believed in entertaining the fans although there were times when referees did not appreciate some of his antics. He hated being beaten and often protested most vehemently to the ref, chasing him back to the centre line. On one occasion he took the ball from the back of his net and followed the ref to the centre line, arguing that the goal was offside. When the ref disagreed with him Albert placed the ball on the centre spot and sat on it to the roaring encouragement of the Notts fans. Not until he had been threatened with "marching orders" did he reluctantly return to his goal — without the ball. Another of his antics was to race out of goal to take throw-ins!

Another of the goalkeeping giants of past days was "Tiny" Joyce, of Millwall and Spurs. He stood well over 6 feet and weighed around 18 stone. He could kick the ball from his own goalmouth into the opposition goal area, and took all his team's penalties. He would start his run downfield from his own goal and without pausing in stride crash the ball into the net. He never missed a spot kick. On one occasion when Spurs were playing a match in France they were awarded a penalty. Tiny Joyce started to amble up the field in his usual style but before he reached the

"Fatty" Foulke stood a cheeky opponent on his head.

halfway line the French goalie thought discretion was better than valour and dashed off the field, scared stiff! That was Tiny's easiest ever penalty!

Here's another amusing story of one of the old-time 'keepers. This time it's Bob Roberts of West Bromwich Albion. When Albion took the field at Nottingham in 1887 for the Cup Semi Final against Preston North End they did so without their goalie. Bob Roberts, a solicitor, had been delayed and had to catch a later train than his team-mates. The game had been going for nearly 10 minutes when the crowd behind the goal parted. The missing 'keeper had arrived wearing his footer togs (including the long white trousers he always wore). He leapt over the fence, dropped his travelling bag behind the net and a few moments later was making his first save. Can you imagine that happening today?

There are hundreds of stories that could be told about players of the past, all of them personalities loved by the fans. Billy Meredith, the long, skinny winger of Manchester City and Wales, never took the field without his "lucky" toothpick clenched between his teeth. Steve Bloomer, one of the greatest inside-forwards of all time, was also superstitious. He played his first game for Derby County at the age of 18 — and scored his first-ever League goal. From then on for the rest of his magnificent career 22 years later he wore only two pairs of boots. Throughout the whole of his career, which brought him 450 goals, 28 of them for England, he religiously wore one pair for the first-half of a match and the other for the second 45 minutes. On one occasion in an important game he had a terrible first-half. Nothing went right. Back in the dressing room for the interval he suddenly turned to the trainer and blamed him for his non success. He had given Steve his SECOND-HALF boots by mistake! Like so many old-time players he was very superstitious, one of the reasons why he always refused to scrap his lucky boots.

If ever there was a crowd loving personality it was Steve Bloomer of the canny skills and uncanny scoring ability. Another was also an inside forward and one of the fantastic little 'uns — incredible Alex James, who cost Arsenal a mere £9,000 from Preston in 1929. The little Scot never looked like a famous footballer when he took the field. He always wore shorts that covered his knees and a shirt that looked far too big for him, but there was magic in his feet. Alex and left-winger Cliff Bastin became just about the greatest attacking partnership in the game, with the wee Scot dazzling and demoralising even the tightest marking defences and Bastin applying the finishing touch in front of goal.

Sheffield Wednesday had a similar pair of wizards when they won the Cup in 1935 — Mark Hooper and Ellis Rimmer. Mark was so small that he always wore "boys" boots, size 4, but he was a wee dazzler with his speed and footwork. When he wasn't scoring goals himself he was supplying inch-perfect passes for Ellis Rimmer to put the ball into the back of the net, although it nearly didn't happen in that exciting Final. Superstition played a part . . .

Before the Third Round of the Cup that season someone presented Ellis Rimmer with a small horseshoe to which was attached a little black cat mascot. From then on before every Cup tie the horseshoe was hung on Rimmer's hook in the dressing-room. But it was not there when the teams changed for the Wembley Final. It had been left at Hillsborough. In the first-half the Wednesday fans wondered what had happened to their favourite winger, who was right out of form. But when the team returned to the dressing-room at the interval there was the lucky mascot hanging on the right hook. One of the Wednesday ground staff had spotted it that morning and rushed to Wembley with it. The magic worked. Mark Hooper scored and Ellis Rimmer hit two, the last the winner. Was it superstition? Who can say.

Back to goalkeeper-personalities of the past. This time it's Gil Merrick of Birmingham City. Gil was almost

Spurs' pocket-sized winger pushed the ball through a defender's legs.

unknown when he took over from that prince of 'keepers Harry Hibbs, one of the greatest England goalies of all time. On the day Harry retired he presented Gil with his old weather-worn cap which had been his constant "companion" throughout his wonderful career. From that day Gil Merrick always took his "mascot" with him on to the field and although he never wore it the cap was placed carefully in the back of the net. Merrick became almost as great an England 'keeper as his predecessor. Did Harry Hibbs' old cap have anything to do with it? Who can tell?

Soccer crowds have always loved men who have provided them with something more than supreme football skills. Call it personality. Men like Sunderland's Len Shackleton, known as the "Clown Prince of Soccer" because of his incredible antics on the field that mesmerised opposing defenders; "Fanny" Walden, tiny winger of Spurs, who once pushed the ball through a big defender's legs, raced round him and carried on down the wing with the ball; Denis Law, pride of the Old Trafford fans and a pain in the neck to opponents; Sir Stanley Matthews with the twinkling feet and wizard ball control, and, of course, Georgie Best during his earlier years. Men like them could pack any football ground because of their individual skills and dominating personalities.

Today there are players of similar ability, perhaps more than ever before, but the game has become too serious and players too stereotyped. Individuals are few and far between — more's the pity.

"Off!" But the 'keeper went on a sit-down strike.

Crystal Palace's Jim Cannon fights off the challenge of Aston Villa's Allan Evans (left) and Kenny Swain.

**TERRY
BUTCHER
Ipswich Town**

Strikers come in all shapes and sizes with all different strengths and weaknesses ... and that's one of the prime reasons goalkeeping is the difficult business it is.

At one time it used to be more predictable but over the years, tactics have obviously improved, teams have got much more variety and goalkeepers are finding that they have to adapt like never before.

When I first came on the scene as a teenager with Leicester, more often than not I was up against a side whose attacking style was built around a big fellow at the front who was good in the air.

Centre-forwards like Ron and Wyn Davies and Tony Hateley come to mind as players who liked the ball tossed up to them to go to work on. And more often than not, there were dividends.

But nowadays, it's all changed. The days of the out and out centre-forward are virtually over and instead of having a six foot-plus target man leading your attack, you've got a quick-moving, quick-thinking striker, who causes endless problems on the floor.

When you think of that type of player, you have got to start with Kenny Dalglish, who, since replacing Kevin Keegan at Anfield, has emerged as such a vital link in the Liverpool attacking machinery.

He's as dangerous with his back to goal as he is coming straight at you because with one feint, one deft flick or one unexpected ball into space, he can set up clear-cut scoring chances for himself and others.

Phil Boyer, now continuing a successful career with Manchester City, is another who is not exactly in the "giant" class but teams he has played for have realised his enormous ability when the ball is played in quickly to him.

He's got this waspish-style that has

him buzzing all over the place, unsettling central defenders and making life uncomfortable for goalkeepers, too.

We still have the big men around, of course, and in the First Division alone there are players who command enormous respect for their ability in the air.

But these days you have to expect much more than sheer physical presence from a central striker. Look at Andy Gray, for example. He's all hustle and bustle and if you need any reminding of the fact, just remember the way he got involved with David Needham and I at Wembley in 1980 in the League Cup Final before side-footing the ball into an empty net after David and I had collided.

Whether it be with Aston Villa, Wolves or Scotland, Andy has never been afraid to take more than his share

'Strikers who make my life extra-difficult'

'Kenny Dalglish — a vital link in the Liverpool attacking machinery'

of knocks and bruises if it meant getting on the end of goalscoring chances.

But there's more to him than that ... much more. He's got a lot of ability on the deck in being able to keep his front line moving by laying off balls quickly and accurately. And, of course, he's got an explosive shot that you have always got to be aware of when he's within firing range.

Justin Fashanu, who has made such remarkable progress for a youngster, is another striker capable of being equally effective when the ball is in the air or on the ground.

His talent was all wrapped up in that memorable goal he scored against Liverpool last season, when the television cameras caught him turning to volley a superb effort out of the reach of Ray Clemence.

That's one instance of a goalkeeper thinking he's got all his options open

'Gary Shaw — scored in successive seasons against me'

and then someone produces a flash of brilliance that you just cannot legislate for.

It happened to me against Birmingham last season when Frank Worthington, who has got tremendous skill, came in at an angle and although I thought I had got my positioning right could do nothing when Frank bent the ball around me and inside the far post. It was a superb goal.

Just going back to the big men for a second, Joe Jordan is recognised as one of the best around at unsettling defences and although you always know it's going to be a physical battle with him, he's another who is often under-rated on the deck.

But, for my money, the best centre forward in the widest sense at the

moment is Ipswich's Paul Mariner. I really have been impressed with the way his all-round game has developed to the benefit of Bobby Robson's team.

He's good in the air; he's got pace; the ability to go past defenders; and the requirement of any striker — to get goals.

Having broken through into the international scene, his game has really blossomed and his partnership with Alan Brazil is one of the key reasons why Ipswich achieved so much last season.

Some managers like their strikers to hunt in pairs. Our own Ian Wallace had a great partnership with Mick Ferguson at Coventry, Frank Stapleton and Alan Sunderland have done so well together at Arsenal and I can see another impressive combination in Peter Withe and Gary Shaw at Aston Villa.

Peter is a phenomenal worker and he's got the all-round attributes that are needed to keep a front line moving. And in young Shaw, he's got the ideal partner to benefit from the openings he creates.

Shaw has scored in successive seasons against me at the City Ground and I've really been impressed with his neatness and ability to sniff out an opportunity.

What's impressed me most about him is his knack of being able to hit the ball early. It's a priceless gift for a striker and a nightmare for goalkeepers, who don't get the time to prepare themselves for a shot the way other strikers permit.

I've seen him strike a ball with virtually no back lift at all — Charlie George is another capable of doing it — and as his progress continues, I can see the Aston Villa youngster making a massive impression in the game.

In an earlier column for "Shoot", I likened him to Allan Clarke, who really did cause goalkeepers problems. The strength of Allan was that he always

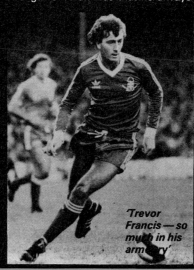

'Trevor Francis — so much in his armoury'

knew where a goalkeeper was most vulnerable.

In one and one situations, I pride myself in having a reasonably good record. Too many goalkeepers rush out and make up a striker's mind for him but I prefer to go so far and then say "come and beat me."

I used to do the same with Allan but he had great ability to weigh up a situation and then crash the ball at your ankles, which is a weak point for any oncoming goalkeeper.

Allan would leave his options open but to be able to do that you have got to have composure and wide-ranging skills, which takes me on to Trevor Francis.

I've played with Trevor and against him, of course, and without doubt he is one of the most exciting strikers in world football. His tremendous pace is such a great asset for any striker but when you are facing him you realise he has got so much more to his armoury.

I remember playing for Forest against Birmingham just before Trevor joined us and he was on the edge of our box with his back to goal. He feinted to go one way, went the other and hit this shot for the top corner. Fortunately, I just managed to get to it and turn it round but it was one of my best saves.

Excite Crowds

Trevor hits a ball so well that he's a danger from two or 20 yards but there was a striker who was just as dangerous from the halfway line!

I'm talking about the incomparable Jimmy Greaves. At the time he was at his peak, Denis Law used to rightly excite crowds with his brilliant finishing inside the box, but Greaves was really outstanding.

I remember one day playing for Leicester at Tottenham and he scored one of the best goals I've ever seen. He took a clearance from his goalkeeper that looked to be going out of play, controlling an impossible ball at the touchline and sweeping past Graham Cross in one movement.

I still didn't think there was a lot of danger with two other defenders between him and me but he waltzed past them, sold me a dummy, and knocked the ball into the net. They were still applauding a couple of minutes later but it was a great goal from a great player, the sort who makes my life between the sticks extra-difficult.

Published by IPC Magazines Ltd., King's Reach Tower, Stamford Street, London SE1 9LS, England.
Sole Agents for Australia and New Zealand: Gordon & Gotch Ltd., South Africa: Central News Agency.
Printed in England by Fleetway Printers, Gravesend, Kent. SBN 85037-671-8

STEVE
BUCKLEY
Derby County